**How Design Makes Us
Think**

How Design Makes Us

Think

Sean Adams

PRINCETON ARCHITECTURAL PRESS, NEW YORK

Published by
Princeton Architectural Press
202 Warren Street
Hudson, New York 12534
www.papress.com

Published in agreement with The Bright Press
© 2021 Quarto Publishing plc
All rights reserved.
Printed and bound in China
24 23 22 21 4 3 2 1 First edition

ISBN: 978-1-61689-972-1 (hardcover)
978-1-61689-977-6 (paperback)

Text and design by Sean Adams

For The Bright Press
Editor: Emily Angus
Picture Researcher: Isabel Zaragoza

For Princeton Architectural Press
Production Editor: Parker Menzimer

Library of Congress Cataloging-in-Publication
Data available upon request.

Opposite:
Exhibition panel from the IBM pavilion ("Think")
New York World's Fair
Charles and Ray Eames
1964

Following:
TR-005 Orbitel television
Panasonic
1972

Contents

Introduction

All design in any media is created to engage the viewer.
Designers use typography, images, form, material, and color to
communicate a message, whether designing a 2D graphic,
automobile, or telephone. The communication is often overt:
"I'm functional as a radio,"[1] or "Visit Australia." Some *covert*
signals and cues also help the viewer form thoughts and
emotions that are less easy to articulate. It may—or may not be—
the goal of the designer to manipulate the viewer's reaction.
Nevertheless, every element in successful design works together
to tell us how to think and, typically, what to do.

1

1
Braun T 1000 Radio
Dieter Rams
1963
Photograph:
Katherine Du Tiel

2
Pyramides de Gizèh
photograph
Gustave Le Gray
1865–69

3
The York Theater
Group poster
Sean Adams
2019

2

Interestingly, when interviewed, most designers are seemingly unaware of the formal tools applied to manipulate a response. One might suggest that he or she added yellow to a poster to make it "happy." Another describes the smooth forms of the vacuum cleaner as "nicer to see." While this may indicate a deficit in the designer's self-awareness or ability to articulate critical thinking, intuition is one of the best designer's greatest tools.

One designer told me that he advises clients that 80 percent of the solution will be based on research, logic, and rational thinking. The remaining 20 percent is intuition. He could not, and would not, attempt to justify this part of a solution. Working intensely in a world of communication driven by the tiniest detail, designers are brilliant at intuitively recognizing the formal issues required to elicit the correct response. Deep experience manipulating form, materials, color, typography, and imagery allows a skilled designer to elicit a reaction from the viewer that is complex and, at times, contradictory.

For example, a children's toy will read as innocent and carefree. But why? What in its form is honestly innocent and playful? We read these attributes into the artifact because we have repeated exposure to similar toys in the context of children. Add some blank zombie-like white eyes to the porcelain doll, and it's evil. The culmination of our experiences and references determine our connection, or lack thereof, to a communication.

Other forms demand that we think. For example, we might ask why there is a bite out of the Apple logo. Or, when we are confronted by the pyramids at Giza, we might ask who built them, how, and why they were built. These questions arise as we feel awe, power, and our sense of smallness against the vast size of the structures. [2]

As another example, consider the poster for a play by James Bullitt, *The Great Basin*. The design suggests that this is not a slapstick comedy. [3] We expect the content

to be cerebral and thought-provoking. Why do we make these assumptions? By deconstructing the elements, we can see how the message is manipulated:

» Bold sans serif typography with a strict asymmetrical flush left layout to tell us that the subject is serious. It is not frivolous or to be considered "light."

» A black-and-white photograph presented with no alteration, such as Photoshop manipulation or color addition tells us that there is no deception. The raw truth will be exposed.

» The white background creates a tone of drama, rather than a black background that, when combined with the stark image, may appear as a horror.

These choices tell the viewer what to expect and entice him or her to attend the theatrical production. In this case, the goal is transparent honesty. If this is your cup of tea, you'll enjoy it. Nobody is pretending there will be dancing and singing cowboys and cowgirls, ranch hands, and a rousing chorus like in *Oklahoma!*.

3

The York
Theater Group
James Bullitt
The Great Basin
The York Theater
June 24–July 5
www.yorktheatergroup.com
6045 W Temple St, Los Angeles, California 90012

4

4
Vase
**California Faience
Pottery Studio**
1920

Or, take the example of a vase from the California Faience pottery studio. First of all, the color is a natural and earthy green; it is not neon or garish. [4] This tells us that the vase is connected to the natural world and is an everyday object. It is not a beautiful piece of French porcelain with hand-painted flowers and aristocrats on swings. Secondly, the form is fluid and straightforward, referencing Japanese pottery rather than European styles. The takeaway for the viewer, regardless of their design experience, is that the vase is friendly, natural, and casual. This is not the vase at your grandmother's house that everyone avoided.

Many forms have explicit cultural significance. The color white in Western society reads as purity. In Eastern culture, it may be considered a symbol of death. Recognizing the genesis and the intended audience is critical to the practice of deconstructing any form of design.

We are surrounded by design. Every part of the man-made world is designed. Often we stop seeing it; it fades into the background, like telephone poles. Ask a non-designer how cereal boxes are made, and he or she will assume a giant cereal box machine pumps out the design.

Recognizing the designer's power to create an emotional response and arouse desire is critical to modern life. As designers it allows us to be more purposeful and aware of the formal choices we make—and our inherent responsibility to do good. For non-designers, it creates a level playing field. One may feel moved to tears after seeing the television commercial of a puppy reunited with a twelve-year-old boy by the river. But now, we will be cognizant of the conscious connection to the characters and symbols we already know from books like *Tom Sawyer* or *Old Yeller*.

There are so many possible emotional and intellectual responses to a given design that it is hard to disentangle them. At one point, I considered the title, *How Design Makes Us Feel*. But that title rejected the rational processes we utilize to accept or refuse a message. The smooth forms of a new office chair feel good emotionally, but we are aware, intellectually, that it will function adequately, not require frequent repair, and project the aura of power we desire.

Marketers and designers are aware that their audience is assaulted by millions of messages daily. And that most people have a rational distrust of many of these messages. To be heard, understood, and remembered, the designer must engage the audience first to attract attention. He or she must then engage the viewer to spend time with the communication or engage with the object. A design must walk the fine line of being easy to use or understand and complex enough to require more attention. And finally, the audience, viewer, or user needs to leave the experience with a positive feeling about the product or design.

Recognizing precisely what reaction we want to create and how to reach that requires more than an intuitive sense of something feeling "happy" or "sad." The following chapters delve into the sociological, psychological, and historical reasons for our responses. I explored these issues as a designer, as I am not a neurologist, psychologist, or sociologist. What visual and conceptual cues resonate, and why? This was my constant question. In the end, how does design make us think?

Chapter 1: Seduction

Seduction is the entry point to an artifact, screen-based solution, or product. If the forms do not seduce the viewer, he or she will not see or interact with the solution. To seduce the viewer is to create a powerful attraction that invites him or her to look more closely and become more intimate with the message. The alternative is to design banal solutions that fail to engage the viewer, or to create repulsive forms, turning the viewer from the communication regardless of the content.

5

6

5
*Krishna and
Radha with Their
Confidantes: Page
from a Dispersed
Gita Govinda*
Painting
Style of Manohar
1655

6
Poster for ArtCenter
Spring Lecture Series
Sean Adams
2019

7
Starbucks logo on cup
**Starbucks and
Lippincott**
2011

7

To understand why we are enticed to interact or concentrate on one form rather than another, it is necessary to explore how we engage with beauty. At the neurological level, the part of our brain involved with aesthetic judgment is within the cerebral cortex, specifically the medial orbitofrontal cortex. This area is believed to be associated with the integration of all senses, determination of value, the expectation of results, and decision making. In other words, it is an area that involves our sense of reward and pleasure.

Donald A. Norman, a cognitive scientist and researcher, posits that a response to an external form integrates three attributes: visceral, behavioral, and reflective design. Visceral design, tied to appearance, is the most deep-seated biological response. To survive as a species, we needed to make quick judgments based on appearances. Bright fruits and a clear blue sky are healthy. Rotting meat and menacing clouds may be unhealthy.

A poster with bright yellow, fresh tulips demands the viewer's attention. [6] The characters, pattern, and color of an Indian watercolor from 1655 invite the viewer to enter the narrative. In this instance, it is a story of seduction, as Krishna holds his hand in a gesture of exposition, while Radha gazes on in erotic expectation. [5]

Behavioral design addresses emotions such as pleasure or disgust based on our experience. A perfectly round wheel will function better than an elliptical one. Subsequently, we prefer the round shape for the wheel, finding it easier to use.

Reflective design also requires more complex thinking: it involves self-image, personal satisfaction, and associations. It is a determining factor in many brands. A consumer purchases a coffee at Starbucks based on his or her satisfaction with the product, positive previous experiences, and self-identity connected with the status of carrying a Starbucks cup. [7]

8
Flower Garden textile
William Morris
1879

9
Cover for AIGA
Communication
Graphics Competition
Catalog
Peter Bradford
1968

8

People prefer easy options. We experience
stress when asked to make a choice. The
less complicated the decision, the more
comfortable we feel. Design that appears
easy to use is more attractive to us than
design that appears complicated. Bright
colors, such as red, blue, and yellow ask less
of the viewer than a complex color such as
olive green. {9}

The primary colors are natural to recognize
and typically connected to "good" things in
our experience: fruit, flowers, and water.
Olive green is more difficult to process: is it
green, avocado, or gray? Like Brussels
sprouts, complex colors are an acquired
taste, as in the example of a beautiful
William Morris textile design. Hence,
children will prefer to use the brightly
colored pencils rather than a range of black,
grey, and beige tones. {8}

For *Eros*, Herb Lubalin reimagined the
erotic magazine. Lubalin rejected the
traditional visual language of pornographic
magazines, with their scantily clad women
on the covers and cheap paper. He adopted
bright colors, easy to understand and
seductive images, and used large areas
of negative space to frame controversial
content in a sophisticated design.

9

10

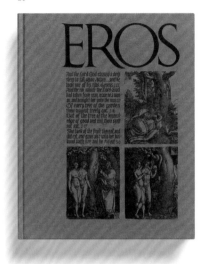

10
Cover of *Eros* magazine
**Herb Lubalin and
John Pistilli**
Winter, 1962

11
Cover of *Eros* magazine
Autumn, 1962

12
Cover of *Eros* magazine
Summer, 1962

11

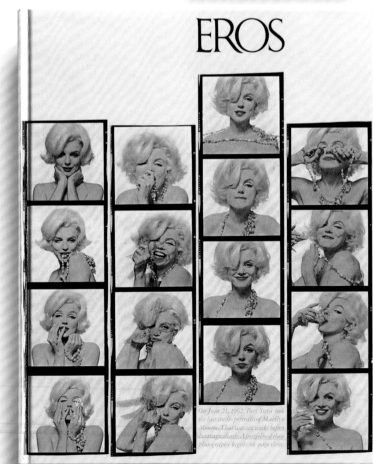

Presenting a range of media from illustration to photography reinforced the alternative aspect of the publication. Lubalin designed the covers to quickly attract the audience and communicate the magazine's content. For an issue about sex and religion, he replaced photographs with a series of medieval woodcuts. [10] And on another cover, breaking from the tradition of refined and airbrushed portraits, he reveals a contact sheet of unretouched images from a Marilyn Monroe photoshoot, including the photographs Monroe attempted to scratch off. [11]

The bright yellow color of another cover displaying an image of a couple engaged in sensual activity attracts the viewer. [12] The overprinted color on a black-and-white photograph and unorthodox cropping of the image, with sand as the primary element, reinforces the message that this is not *Playboy* magazine. Lubalin also discarded the "sell lines" found on a typical magazine cover. Sell lines alert the viewer to the content: "Lose weight in ten days," and other dramatic statements. *Eros*'s lack of sell lines and hardbound binding are typical of a book rather than a magazine. These features work together to create a sense of higher value and longevity—people rarely throw away books.

14

13

The graphic system for the 1984 Summer Olympics reintroduced Los Angeles to the world as a vibrant and forward-thinking community. Los Angeles had recently been painted as a grim city of brown smog, earthquakes, and traffic jams. The noted Los Angeles-based designer, Deborah Sussman, discarded a corporate international style approach to the Olympics and worked with a bright, pure, and bold palette to further the communication.

The simple geometric shapes, sans serif typography, and postmodern forms referred to a Memphis or New Wave aesthetic. Both movements were popular during the 1980s with artists, musicians, architects, and designers. The graphic approach signified new energy, technology, and a connection to a vibrant Southern California culture. [13, 14]

The rainbow hues of the architecture at the Saguaro Hotel in Palm Springs create a proprietary tone for the resort and communicate the brand message. [15] Here, the idea is to convey a youthful, casual, and energetic experience. The Saguaro Hotel is clearly not a hotel where guests are required to dress formally for dinner, but a resort for loud music and mai tai cocktails.

13
Design Quarterly 127:
LA 84: Games of the
XXIII Olympiad
publication
Deborah Sussman
1985

14
LA84: Games of the
XXIII Olympiad
environmental graphic
system
Deborah Sussman and
Jerde Partnership
1983

15
Saguaro Hotel,
Palm Springs
Stamberg Aferiat
Architecture
2016

15

16
Golden section and
golden rectangle

17
Hurricane Lester
on approach to
Hawaii with golden
section overlay
**NASA image by
Jeff Schmaltz**
2016

18, 19
Poster for UCLA
Extension with and
without golden section
overlay
Sean Adams
2004

16

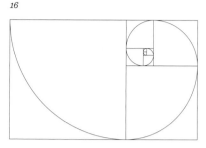

17

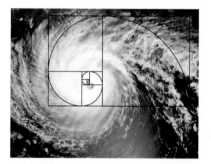

18

Form is a primary element within the context of seduction and visceral design. There are specific shapes we naturally find attractive. As an example, the Greeks believed the golden rectangle to be the most pleasing of forms. [16] The golden section is often referred to as sacred geometry. Characters in books and movies that revolve around conspiracies might uncover a hidden message leading to vital information related to the golden rectangle.

However, the shape and mathematics involved are no secret. Most designers and architects are well-versed on golden rectangle proportions. The mathematics, based on the Fibonacci sequence, recur with impossible frequency woven in nature, in the shape of galaxies, hurricanes, plants, and the human body. [17] Mathematically, the ratio is approximately 1 to 1.618.

The Greeks designed buildings based on the golden rectangle. Leonardo Da Vinci applied it to *Mona Lisa, The Last Supper,* and many of his paintings. Notre Dame is a series of golden rectangles. In modern design, Oscar Niemeyer, Le Corbusier, and Wallace Harrison worked with the shape on the United Nations headquarters. Most computer screens are a golden rectangle.

Adrian Bejan, J. A. Jones Distinguished Professor at Duke University, theorizes that the human eye is capable of interpreting an image featuring the golden ratio more efficiently than any other. He theorizes that we evolved scanning the horizontal plane for threats and food, and subsequently, the shape is the best configuration for images for fast transmission and recognition by the brain.

The golden section serves as the basis for an underlying structure to create harmony in design. My poster for UCLA Extension's winter quarter embraces the golden section as a compositional guide. [18, 19] The golden ratio proportions determine the shape of the poster, the position and scale of the surfboard shapes and typography, and the negative space.

The graphic designer Paul Rand said, "A good logo cannot make a bad product good. Nevertheless, a good logo can make a good product great." This translates to another metaphor: "Putting lipstick on a pig doesn't make it not a pig." Subsequently, many design solutions, be they graphic, product, packaging, or screen-based, rely on a visceral response to appearance alone to seduce and engage the viewer.

19

20

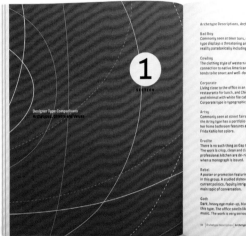

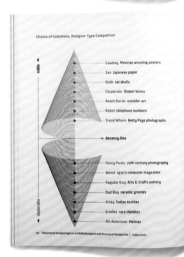

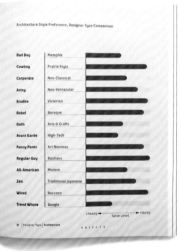

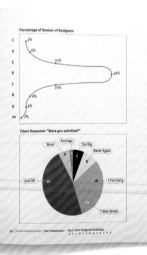

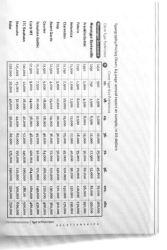

20
Designologicus 13
publication
Sean Adams
2004

A beautiful surface design that attracts the viewer to read the content, buy the product, or engage with the screen is the only option when the content is questionable. When the subject matter repulses, bores, or challenges the viewer, the designer may create a solution that borrows the appearance of a different message so that it will be accepted.

To explore the concept of deceiving by appearance, I gave the book *Designologicus 13* a veneer of in-depth research and information design. I created charts, graphs, and diagrams with multiple axes and types of information. A simple black and red color palette, a liberal application of hairline rules, and small, clinical typography reinforced the official and scientific validity and tenor of the content. [20]

The result was a book that superficially appeared to be composed of in-depth research and critical information. However, lacking the time and expertise to create a wide-reaching sociological study, I created fictional content. The information was shallow and irreverent, and included lists of favorite sunglasses, shoes, and hobbies.

The book won multiple awards, and designers congratulated me on producing a sociological study of the design population. The intent was not to deceive, but to highlight disparity between the appearance of a design solution and actual content.

On a less primal level, the viewer will examine an object, communication, or machine and determine, from appearance, if it is pleasurable and easy to use or challenging and stressful. We prefer the former and are seduced by the possible enjoyment in using the object.

Consider the telephone as an example of industrial design. The designers responsible for the 1907 Magneto Wall Set telephone and 1919 Western Electric Dial Phone created solutions that are efficient and easy to use, though they require two hands. As one of the first home telephones, the user might be unsure of the operation of the contraption. The goal of first the wooden box, then the black candlestick's industrial appearance was not to seduce the viewer to operate the telephone but to simply convey that it worked. [21, 22]

21

22

23

24

25

26

27

21	**23**	**25**	**27**
Magneto Wall Set	Hungarian Telephone	500 Type Color	Princess Phone
Western Electric	Factory telephone	Desk Set	**Henry Dreyfuss and**
1907	**Telefongyár**	**Henry Dreyfuss**	**Donald Genaro**
	1937	1954	1959

22	**24**	**26**	**28**
Dial Telephone	500 Type Desk Set	Wall Telephone	iPhone 8
Western Electric	**Henry Dreyfuss**	**Henry Dreyfuss**	**Apple, Inc.**
1919	1949	1961	2017

28

Later telephone models such as the 1937 Hungarian Telephone Factory telephone refined the forms to work better on a desk and in one's hand. [23] The Hungarian Telephone Factory telephone appears easy to operate, but is still a commercial industrial tool.

Five years later, Henry Dreyfuss's 1949 Western Electric 500 Type Desk Set and color option softened the form of the telephone for home use and added pleasant color tones. [24, 25] The addition of a Wall Telephone addressed the desire for a telephone in the kitchen. [26] These designs communicate the effortlessness and delight of operation.

The Princess Phone, designed and marketed for teenage girls and women, raises issues of aesthetic choices based on gender. [27] Gender assumptions of the 1950s stated that women preferred pleasing color and soft forms. The name, Princess Phone, is addressed to teenage girls. How can a yellow telephone with an added brass handle cover be anything but easy to use and lovely in a pastel pink bedroom? The more significant issue here is whether these aesthetic preferences are inherent or learned by repeated exposure from an early age.

29
Perfume decanter
**New England Glass
Company**
1866–70

The iPhone [28] is a remarkably simple form. It is an undemanding rectangle (incorporating the golden ratio) with no apparent moving parts or appendages. [28] It fits comfortably in the palm of the user's hand, creating a personal connection. The surface materials, metal and glass, are smooth and elegant. As an object alone, it is a tiny *2001: A Space Odyssey* monolith.

The interface is the design element that seduces the user with the message of straightforward operation. Here, technology is not scary or complicated to understand. Brightly colored icons organized in an accessible grid invite the user to engage. The albums of photographs add a personal connection to the device. The phone succeeds where other mobile phones failed, not by signaling that it was the most high-tech and advanced option, but by projecting the message that it is the easiest to operate.

The iPhone is also a perfect example of the third aspect of beauty and seduction, our self-image. It is not an inexpensive object. The materials are not plastic or gaudy but sophisticated and understated. It is an elegant piece of industrial design that tells others, "I know quality and do not need

to be showy." By associating ourselves with the positive perceptions of the Apple brand, and the recognition that we can afford a costly item, we reinforce our status to others.

Value is a component of seduction that connects to how we identify ourselves and connect to the external world. Our environment and culture determine value. One may assign value to an expensive European car while a member of an ascetic religious order might find it distasteful and an example of excess. We value things our community has assigned as good. We are seduced to spend large amounts of money on small quantities of perfume. The packaging, bottle design, and scent send the signal to others that we can afford luxury. [29]

Finally, memory and idealization seduce us. Maxfield Parrish's illustration, *Daybreak*, suggests a natural pastoral scene of a romanticized landscape. [30] Another image, *Sleeping Beauty in the Wood*, depicts a scene from the fairy tale. The golden sunset lighting and lush fabrics convey rest and comfort.

Well-maintained flowers in pots and the Grecian tone of columns and clothing add a veneer of safety and reassurance in the man-made environment. [31]

In a society that values these ideas, the viewer is engaged. He or she then imagines him or herself in that environment. Maxfield Parrish carefully arranged these forms and masterfully managed the effect of light to attract the reader and communicate the message on this illustration for editorial use.

Seduction involves several emotions that range from automatic responses to elaborate thinking. Designers integrate color, form, imagery, material, and context to entice the viewer into the initial communication. The style captivates the viewer. Now the content makes a command.

The audience is asked to assign a set of values to a brand, purchase the item, or take action. We evaluate the form and message and then decide if we will engage with the communication or ignore it. Successful solutions first attract the viewer and then connect with the messages of ease of use while simultaneously providing the user with a positive self-image.

29

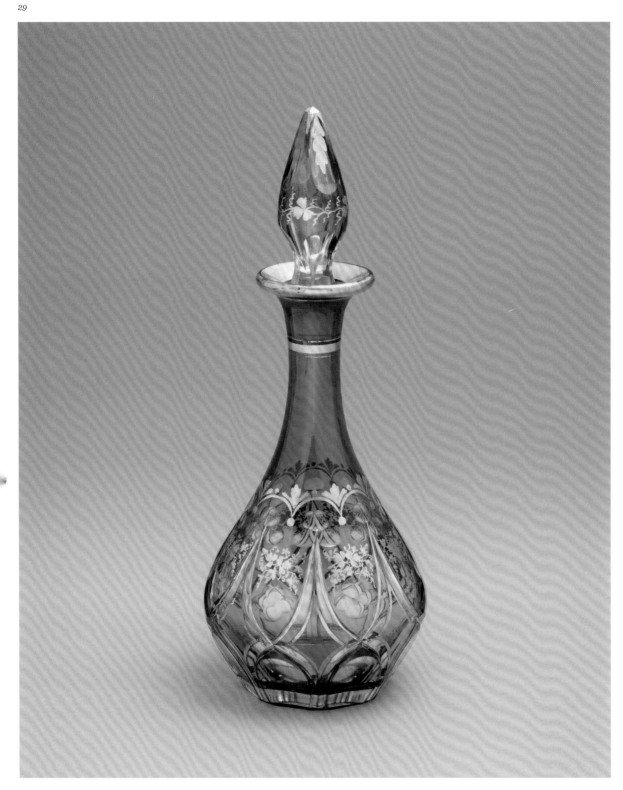

30
Daybreak
Maxfield Parrish
1929

31
*Sleeping Beauty in
the Wood*
Maxfield Parrish
1912

30

31

Chapter 2: Efficiency

We determine efficiency based on the necessary resources to produce the desired result. How much time, energy, and thought are required to operate a product or understand a message? When the effort outweighs the result, we reject the object, and it fails. Imagine a poster that is overly complex with diminutive and illegible typography, or a ceiling lamp that is impossible to operate. If deeply engaged, the viewer may take time to understand the content or figure out how to turn on the light. However, if the viewer is casually interested, and the resources necessary to understand the design outweigh the result, then the viewer will ignore the poster and purchase the efficient and straightforward ceiling lamp. {32}

32

32
DMB 26 Pendant Lamp
Marianne Brandt
1926

33
Bauhaus Dessau
window detail
Walter Gropius
1925

34
Bauhaus Dessau
building
Walter Gropius
1925

33

The industrial revolution led to us to place high value on efficient design. As society moved from an agrarian to urban experience and machinery replaced human activity, we increasingly appreciated efficient design to improve our lives. A practical product allows the user to exert less energy and spend less time on a task, and subsequently leads to more leisure time for the user.

When a product or communication works well and efficiently, we enjoy the engagement. The plastic packaging for a USB flash drive that requires multiple knives, scissors, and hand strength to access the product fails. The frustrated owner has a negative perception of the brand and is furious and agitated before touching the actual flash drive. Conversely, a brand succeeds when the design suggests ease of use and when its function matches these expectations.

In the 1920s, designers and architects at the Bauhaus placed a premium on function. Based on the mistrust of the aristocracy and devastation of World War I, these designers rejected ornamentation and unnecessary decoration as symbols of corruption. Their idea was that a designer should focus on function before form and style. These designers believed society would function with harmony if we all used the same teapot and valued it for effective operation rather than "impure" elaborate decoration.

Walter Gropius designed the Bauhaus in Dessau in 1925 as a "machine for learning." Gropius rejected the forms of traditional academia, Greek columns, marble-clad temples, and ivy-covered walls, in favor of exposed metal and a glass curtain for the exterior. [34] The windows opened mechanically to showcase the machine-like structure. [33] Students lived in identical rooms at the dormitory designed for functionality. Uniform living spaces would diminish social hierarchy and envy, creating an egalitarian culture.

Two decades after the Nazi regime closed the Bauhaus Dessau, Ludwig Mies van der Rohe, the school's last director, designed the Edith Farnsworth House in Plano, Illinois. [35, 36] Mies van der Rohe made aesthetic choices to prioritize function. Modernist tenets, such as truth in materials, are apparent with the exposed metal beams and building structure. Like at the

34

35

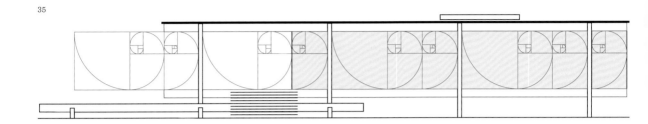

36

35
Edith Farnsworth
House elevation with
golden rectangle

36
Edith Farnsworth House
**Ludwig Mies van der
Rohe**
1951
Photographer:
Carol Highsmith

37
Card for Pan Am
Cargo Schedule
**Chermayeff &
Geismar**
c. 1965

38
Pan Am Cargo
Schedule with
golden section
overlay

37

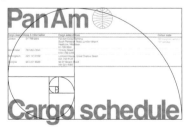

38

Bauhaus Dessau, in the Edith Farnsworth
House, Mies van der Rohe used vast
expanses of glass for the exterior. This
blurred the lines between the interior
and exterior and created a wallpaper of
natural landscape.

The house's functionality is meant to be
apparent: the building is mostly transparent, there is nothing hidden. The open plan
of the interior is flexible for usage. However,
Mies van der Rohe did not design for pure
functionality. Following his philosophy of
the necessity for human beings to connect
with nature, while recognizing the era of
industrial mass production, Mies van der
Rohe stated, "We should attempt to bring
nature, houses, and the human being to a
higher unity." He embedded proportions
such as the golden section and worked
with a simple palette of materials. {35}
The architecture communicates openness
and function in a natural landscape. {36}

Even the most mundane projects demanded
modernism's goal of efficiency and harmony. Chermayeff and Geismar applied the
same rigor to all elements from travel
posters to a simple cargo manifest from
PanAm. {37 & 38}

39
Tea Infuser and
Strainer
teapot
Marianne Brandt
1924

40
Dessau: Alter Kultur,
NeuesArbeitsstätten
brochure
Herbert Bayer
1926

41
Universal Type
typeface
Herbert Bayer
1926

40

39

41

abcdefghi
jklmnopqrs
tuvwxyz
1234567890

42
Eames Chaise Lounge
Charles and Ray Eames
1968

43
Europe: United States Lines poster
Lester Beall
1953

44
Catalog for and exhibition of photographs by Blake Little
Sean Adams
2017

45
Bell System logo
Saul Bass
1957

42

43

44

Blake Little's twist on these various embodiments of virility comes in the fact that all of the subjects are gay men. "Little's authentic documentation of a new gay masculine subculture continues as he pushes his portraiture in different ways.

His visual vocabulary has evolved from the more formal structure of his earlier pictures, taking more chances and benefiting from this basic freedom."

EUROPE

NEW S.S. UNITED STATES · S.S. AMERICA
UNITED STATES LINES

45

46

Typographic system

English typography
Typeface   Helvetica Neue LT Std 75 Bold
Type size   Any of the specified sizes

Japanese typography
Typeface   Hiragino Kakugo Std W8
Type size   85%

For both languages
Leading   100%
Kerning   Optical *
Tracking   -35 *
Justification   (info on separate page) *
Alignment   Left aligned

* Settings in Adobe InDesign
Please refer to info on separate page

For example:
Within the same text block
Helvetica Neue LT Std 75 Bold
18/18 pt
Hiragino Kakugo Std W8
15.3/18 pt

Naming structure

1. 'Askul' in English

2. **Product name in English**   Product name: Garbage Bag

3. **Product name + attribute (if any)**   Product name: Garbage Bag
    in Japanese   Attribute: Refill

4. **Product specifications in Japanese**   Specifications: 100 sheets/pad
    (size, weight, quantity, colour etc.)   50 pieces
                                                             45 L

**Askul
Garbage bag
ゴミ袋・詰替用
半透明
50枚・45L**

Information block structure

D   Information block
E   Information block
    In this case more detailed
    than the Information Block D

1   Line to seperate the information
2   Article Numbers
3   Information Text (name, quantity etc.)
4   Line to seperate the information
5   Pictogram
6   Line to seperate the information
7   Barcode

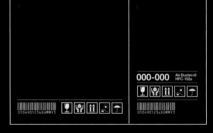

47

46, 47
Identity system and
packaging for Askul
Stockholm Design Lab
2016

For the majority of the twentieth century, designers worked with modernist principals, following, to celebrate function, efficiency, and new technologies.

Geometric Perfection
Bauhaus student Marianne Brandt removed all decoration and various materials on her Samovar to favor functionality and pure geometry. {39}.

New Technology
Another Bauhaus student Herbert Bayer designed a brochure for the city of Dessau, displaying the ornate traditional city hall. But Bayer added new machines: an airplane and the Bauhaus campus. The modern elements and sharp geometric forms reinforce the message of Dessau as a center of old culture and new workplaces. {40}

Simplicity
Bayer also designed a typeface that simplified the letterforms with geometry. He eliminated capital letters to create a more egalitarian concept with no inherent political hierarchy. {41} There is no italic font nor additional weights; these decisions simplify the options for a user.

Form Follows Function
Film director Billy Wilder enjoyed daily naps limited to fifteen minutes. Friends Charles and Ray Eames designed a chaise lounge for Wilder to assist with the fifteen-minute rule. The chaise has a narrow profile. If Wilder began to sleep longer, his arms would fall to his side and wake him. The base is exposed and honest, the form follows the function of short napping. {42}

Dynamic Asymmetry
Lester Beall's poster for United States Lines rejected the expected cruise-line visual vernacular of luxurious destinations. Instead, he adopted Bauhaus typographic models and asymmetric layout. Like Bayer's Dessau brochure, Beall incorporated sans serif typography, minimal color, and geometric forms to communicate speed and efficiency. {43}

Less is More
The catalog for an exhibition of photographer Blake Little's work communicates strength with simple black-and-white color and a minimal typographic palette of one typeface in one weight and size. The reductive approach creates a minimal canvas for Little's images. {44}

Good Design For the Masses
When The Bell Telephone Company asked Saul Bass to update their logo to communicate their position as the communications leader of tomorrow, Bass simplified the illustrative forms of the logo with a consistent line size and circular shapes. Bass recognized that a logo should be an iconic symbol, not an illustration of the product. {45}

Rejection of Decoration
One of design's most complex tasks is to create order from chaos. A cohesive and memorable graphic system will create brand visibility and communicate confidence and efficiency. Askul is a Japanese company that delivers supplies within twenty-four hours. The customer values the simplicity in ordering almost any item needed with swift delivery.

For Askul, Stockholm Design Lab designed a holistic, comprehensive, and bold system that organizes over forty thousand different products. {46, 47} The simple forms, limited and cohesive color palette, and sans serif typeface communicate an Apollonian clarity and minimize the stress of decision-making for the customer.

48
Freitag Individual
Recycled Freeway Shop
**spillmann echsle
architekten**
2006
Photographer:
Roland Tännler

The Askul packaging conveys the same level of quality for the rubber bands, batteries, staples, and any other office item. The packaging works together with a unified and vibrant homogeneity. The consumer needs only to consider one source for everything required rather than devote hours of research to an unorganized disorder of thousands of products.

Resources, sustainable practices, and climate change are connected. Efficiency and resources are related. When a designer creates a solution that functions admirably with minimal means, we consider it to be a success. Any design solution, regardless of the quality that requires an excess of toxic materials, is no longer efficient.

Freitag is a brand committed to a circular, closed-loop economy: share, lease, reuse, refurbish, and recycle. Their product, bags created with used truck tarpaulins, discarded bicycle inner tubes, and car seat belts, demonstrates their commitment. The bags are efficient, as they support sustainable practices, but also are weatherproof, durable, unique, and functional.

Freitag's Zurich flagship store proves its dedication to reuse and sustainability. Architects Annette Spillmann and Harald Echsle designed the store with nineteen used steel dry shipping containers as the structure. {48} The architects chose the containers in Hamburg and shipped them to Zurich. Fortunately, the location is next to a major railroad hub where the shipping containers were delivered.

In the space, the customer must set aside preconceptions of a retail environment and embrace the industrial aesthetic. It is, however, that conflict between the expected zen-like atmosphere of a retail store and the unorthodox and raw Freitag space that forces the visitor to see and experience efficiency and reuse as beauty.

Function in design may seem to address only the practical needs of the user or viewer. However, usability, performance, effectiveness, and sustainability create a positive emotion. When a design solution succeeds, the viewer feels connected and confident. An efficient solution builds trust, and therefore engenders repeated actions.

49
Advertisement for
Volkswagen:
("It's ugly, but it
gets you there.")
Doyle Dane Bernbach
1970

50
*Buzz Aldrin with
Apollo 11 Lunar
Module on the Moon*
photographer
Neil Armstrong
1969

51
NASA logo
**Danne and
Blackburn**
1974

After the success of Apollo 11 landing on
the moon, the Lunar Module acquired a
sense of dynamism and romance. But, the
vehicle was far from elegant. An advertisement for a Volkswagen Beetle displayed the
Lunar Module only, and the tagline read,
"It's ugly, but it gets you there." {49}

Our positive association with the Apollo
Lunar Module has little to do with the
design of the ship. It is the emotional
connection, the memory, and pride at the
success of the mission that creates
communication. If the mission had failed,
we would consider the craft merely ugly
and flawed. However, it landed safely; Neil
Armstrong and "Buzz" Aldrin walked on
the moon. The LM successfully rendez-
voused with the Columbia and the
astronauts returned to Earth safely.
Therefore, the LM is remembered as an
efficient and well-designed machine.

Association and memory add to the
message of efficiency. The Apollo Lunar
Module worked and was celebrated. {50}
But it was not elegant visually. It's industrial, awkward, and complicated form was
incapable of flight in earth's atmosphere,
not designed for beauty, but suited for the
vacuum of space.

Richard Danne and Bruce Blackburn's logo
for NASA is a prime example of the power
of positive emotion from the perception of
efficiency and success. {51} Formally, the
logo embraces a modern and fluid form that
communicates strength and precision. If
Danne designed the logo with sharp edges,
the result would be reliable but dangerous
and foreboding.

The genius here is Danne's geometrically
precise rounded corners and bold red color.
There is no superfluous or unnecessary
decoration. The logo and accompanying
graphic system communicate the virtues of
efficiency, accuracy, and power.

As consumers of products and information,
we recognize efficiency with visual cues:
sans serif typography reads as clinical and
precise. {52} As physical beings, weight, and
surface matter to us. Lightweight and
portable imply ease of use and functionality. {53} Black and white convey the idea of
minimal resources and maximum efficiency. {54} Furthermore, graphic and simplified
iconography communicates speed and
universality in communication. In an
airport or railroad station one has no time
to waste searching for the bar, hence the
stripped-down efficiency of the icon. {55}

49

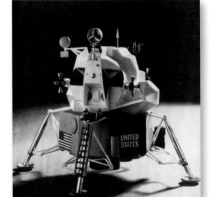

It's ugly, but it gets you there.

51

NASA

50

NASA
AS11-4-4927

52

54

53

55

52
Neue Grafik magazine
Carlo Vivaerlli
1963

53
Polaroid Land
Camera 1000
Polaroid Corporation
1977

54
5:00 Wall Clock
Tibor Kalman
1984

55
AIGA Symbol Set
**Roger Cook and
Don Shanosky**
1974

56
Nelson Miniature
Chest
George Nelson
1952

57
A Subway Poster Pulls
advertisement
**Edward McKnight
Kauffer**
1947

56

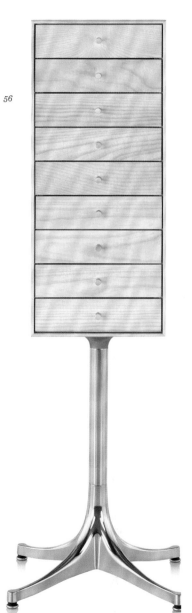

57

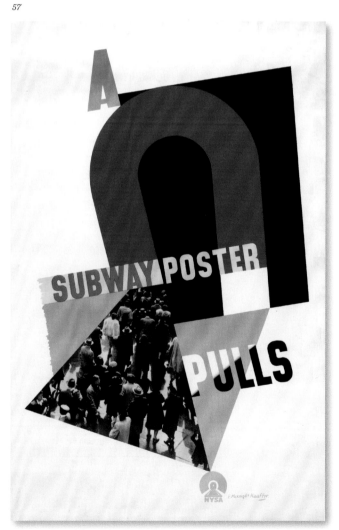

58
8 bar version of the
IBM logo
Paul Rand
1972

59
IBM Plex Sans
Medium typeface
Mike Abbink
2018

58

59

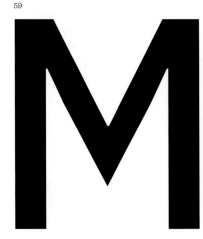

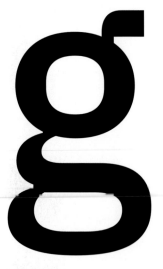

A minimal palette of materials, exposed structure, and lack of ornamentation communicate the rejection of anything that does not contribute to the function. {56} Asymmetrical layout is associated with modernity and usability. {57}

Appreciation of the aesthetics of effectiveness is an acquired taste. Often, as seen with the Lunar landing module, the design is less than graceful, but we recognize the value of the machine. In contemporary culture, we expect a certain level of visual discord. It is challenging to prioritize function and add elaborate gilding and decorative elements. One expects to see the severity, utility, and celebration of the machine with efficiency.

In 1955, when Paul Rand designed the IBM logo, corporate America valued power, stability, and efficient organization. The logo is dynamic and, like the NASA wordmark, precise. {58} It speaks to mathematics, technology, and geometry. The stripes add visual interest, and the sharp point of the *M* provides a focal point

Similarly, the typeface IBM Plex Sans, designed by Mike Abbink, borrows from IBM's history with elements such as the pointed *M* or the use of the IBM Selectric typewriter *G*. {59} The typeface brilliantly communicates IBM's combination of humanity and technology. Abbink designed it for on-screen media and print. It is not dramatic nor pretentious, unlike a classical serif typeface. There is an obvious connection to digital and mechanical technology, and also including a warm touch.

Modernism defines our perception of efficiency. For a century, designers prioritized efficacy along with simplicity and honesty. The best solutions combined reliability and functionality with a visual approach that is true to the product or object's purpose. Today, the promise of efficiency must pair with sustainable practices. No design solution is successful if it ends life in a garbage dump. But, a graceful and refined design that encourages ongoing usefulness is an extraordinary success.

ABCDEFGHIJ
KLMNOPQRS
TUVWXYZ
abcdefghij
klmnopqrs
tuvwxyz
1234567890

Chapter 3: Love

Communicating the concept of love is hard. Love is a multilayered emotion that challenges definition. An individual sees love through his or her kaleidoscope. Love can be about a person, animal, place, idea, or artifact. Designers approach it with metaphor and complexity, or literal cues. {60} Regardless of the conceptual and formal tactic, the communication must connect the message on an emotional level closest to one's identification with the emotion of love. The combination of an inherent emotion combined with memory and association creates a dynamic mnemonic. It is no surprise that brands aspire to inject love into their message: "I'm lovin' it," "Virginia is for lovers," and "I ❤ NY."

60

61

60
International Love
Heart wall relief
Alexander Girard
1965

61
Two Tahitian Women
painting
Paul Gauguin
1899

62
Ugolino and His Sons
sculpture
Jean-Baptiste Carpeaux
1865

62

The biological anthropologist Dr. Helen Fisher explains love with three states of emotion and specific heteronormative biological goals. First, erotic love is the libido, the rush of excitement one may experience connected to the reproductive process. Second, romantic love is an evolutionary development that focuses the attention on one individual. It is a state similar to obsessive-compulsive disorder, creating a dynamic that allows for reproduction. And finally, attachment creates the stable and long-term relationship necessary for child-rearing.

The restrictive morals of the nineteenth century required love as appropriate only within a defined family structure or as a representation of the virginal and pure. No civilized man or woman would make their neighbor or guest at a dinner party an object of erotic desire. One was required to sublimate the base emotion of lust. The exotic and foreign, therefore, provided a license for the idea of the erotic, romantic, and dangerous.

In 1891, Paul Gauguin traveled to Tahiti to paint the local people. [61] In this setting, apart from the world of European morals, he explored the sensual and exotic. That work is an example of the acceptance of nudity in the context of "the other."

Similarly, Jean-Baptiste Carpeaux's sculpture, *Ugolino and His Sons,* allows for the representation of male nudity [62] with its mythical characters from canto XXXIII of Dante's *Inferno.* Therefore, they are separate from daily reality, exempt from the moral rigidity of the period.

The rise of the arts and crafts movement in the late nineteenth century reinforced a fascination with medieval subjects and ideas of chivalry. Aubrey Beardsley's illustrations for *Le Morte d'Arthur*, the story of King Arthur, included natural forms and sensuality not acceptable twenty years earlier. The characters are, again, fictional, and therefore allowed to inhabit a world of lust and adultery. The style of the images with sweeping vines and high contrast broke from the saccharine images of love at the time. [63]

63
Le Morte d'Arthur,
How Queen Guenever
Made Her a Nun
illustration
Aubrey Beardsley
1893–94

64
Reine de Joie
color lithograph
Henri de Toulouse-
Lautrec
1892

Another example of the relaxation of restraints is Henri de Toulouse-Lautrec's poster promoting the novel, *Reine de Joie, moeurs du demi-monde* (*Queen of Joy, The World of Easy Virtue*). [64] The book's plot involves the relationship between an older banker based on Alphonse de Rothschild and a young Parisian courtesan.

The poster depicts a scene in the book. The banker agrees to pay fifty thousand francs a month in addition to gifts of jewelry and a large townhouse to the courtesan. She embraces him with gratitude. The novel asks questions about anti-Semitic attitudes in nineteenth-century Paris. Lautrec, however, presents the scene as a moment of intimacy, disregarding the monetary exchange or issues of age. The red dress and bold tones of the courtesan contrast with the dull green outline of the banker to convey the vitality of youth and love.

Alphonse Marie Mucha connected desire, forbidden love, and romance to exoticism and the external. Mucha was commissioned to illustrate the *La Plume* calendar by the editor Leon Deschamps. Mucha surrounds the subject with the iconography of the zodiac, an occult and titillating subject. In this non-domestic setting, the

63

64

65

66

viewer can safely recognize the figure's sensual elements without risk of "sullying" the reputation of a "decent" woman. [65]

Conversely, in Japan, nudity and representations of the erotic were not categorically deemed indecent in art. However, the Japanese public did not consider a photograph to be "art." The art director Toshiro Kataoka chose opera singer Masushima Emiko as the model for an advertisement for port wine. The enticing gaze and seemingly nude model challenged the established norms of depictions of intimacy. This is an actual person, not an illustration of a fictional character. For a modern viewer, the advertisement seems innocent. But the use of a new media, photography, the minimal background with no decoration, and the direct gaze of a recognizable subject indicated a dramatic shift in accepted conventions. [66]

During most of the nineteenth century, until the late twentieth century, designers communicated one or more of the three acceptable states of love: eros, romance, and attachment. With the advent of the beat movement and counterculture of the 1950s and 1960s, the idea of expressions of love expanded. Love can connect to sexual

67

68

independence, a political statement of
power, erotic exploration, and long-term
attachments separate from biological
reproduction. Communication and design
introduced individuals outside the traditional nuclear family definition or the
heteronormative definition of love.

Love is more than walking with bare feet on
the beach with a partner, enjoying soft
music together, and sitting across from
each other gazing adoringly at dinner. If one
enjoys these things, he or she may continue
to do so. But this kind of portrayal of love in
romantic terms is typically overwrought,
sentimental, melodramatic. {68}

Roy Kuhlman's cover for a paperback of
Hiroshima Mon Amour succeeds in
presenting erotic love and passion. {67} It
does this, not with an explicit image, but
with a soft and grainy film still. The lack of
clear information invites the viewer to
insert him or herself into the scene. With no
apparent cues of recognition, one can
imagine the experience personally. The red
overprint of the image formally adds a bold
color to be seen among the other books in a
bookstore. It also tells the viewer that this
is about passion. It is not sweet and

69
Burning Settlers
Cabin poster
Sean Adams
2014

70
Lorca: 3 Tragedies
book cover
Alvin Lustig
1949

69

innocent adoration. The raw imagery, straightforward typography, and red tell us that this is concerned with adult love with all its inherent complexities.

While Kuhlman's cover communicates the convolution of love, Alvin Lustig's cover for Federico García Lorca's collection of plays, *3 Tragedies*, is a masterpiece of multiple narratives. {70} One individual image could not convey the profundity of Lorca's work. Lustig juxtaposes five discrete images: the moon, ocean waves, handwriting in the sand, a crumpled handwritten note, and a simple cross. Each of these presents multiple narrative options.

One person's perception of the moon may be lunacy, while another may see romance. The ocean waves might explore either emotional depth or sexual power. Handwriting in the sand might be about the impermanence of a light summer's day at the beach. The notepaper demands the questions: who crumpled it, where was it discarded, and who retrieved it? And finally, the cross is clearly about Christianity, but its lack of ornamentation might be associated with a socioeconomic status or vow of poverty.

70

71

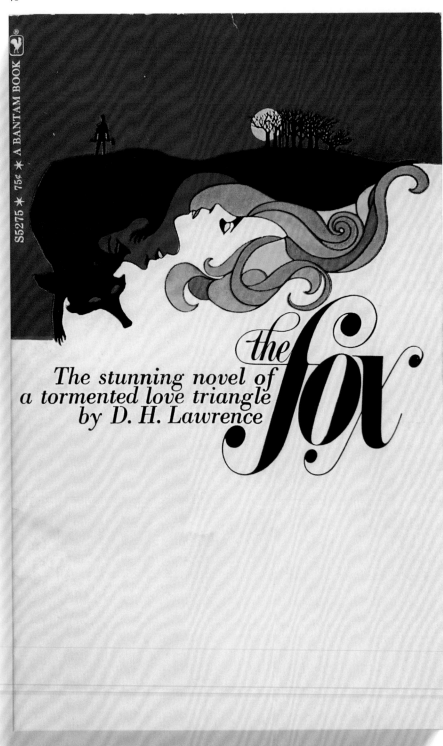

71
Cover for the
paperback edition
of *The Fox*
Diane and Leo Dillon
1967

72, 73
Theurel & Thomas
retail and identity
design
Anagrama
2007

72

As human beings, we tell ourselves stories. It is a biological necessity developed with evolution. Rather than seeing a lion hiding in the tall grass and only recognizing the object, (i.e., thinking only "There is a lion.") we can create a narrative based on experience and knowledge. We imagine the story of that lion leaping from the grass and eating one of us. And we flee accordingly.

Lustig allows the viewer to combine the images into whatever story he or she creates. However, the photos he chose lead the viewer to associations with love, tragedy, emotion, and religion. The message is universal, and love is emotional, contradictory, and far from simple.

Multiple images combine to create numerous stories with contradictions. Any combination of imagery will demand we make sense of the pairing. On a poster to promote a publication, filmic images from Federico Fellini's *8 1/2* and Chris Marker's *La Jetée* add a narrative from the respective plots. The subtitles, referring to burning cabins and settlers, combined with the films' plots and viewer's interpretation multiplies the connections of private narratives and emotions surrounding love as a concept. {69}

By the late 1960s, society moved closer to the relaxation of gender roles and the need for obfuscation of desire and expressions of love. The paperback novel cover and matching film poster for D.H. Lawrence's novella, *The Fox*, explores sexuality, violence, masculinity, and femininity. {71} The illustrators, Diane and Leo Dillon, present the sensual and emotional triangle in the narrative.

The lesbian relationship is openly stated here, with no attempt at sanitizing or hiding it. The position of the two women, seemingly asleep, is threatened by the masculine figure standing with an ax. The fluid letterforms of the title weave together seductively. Even the choice of the secondary typeface, Bodoni italic, with high contrast and delicate forms, adds to the tone of duality and passionate emotions. What might have been a seedy and cheap exploitation of a titillating subject is handled with exquisite skill.

73

74

74
Valentine card with
foil stamp
Marian Bantjes
2018

75
Valentine card with
over-printing
Marian Bantjes
2012

75

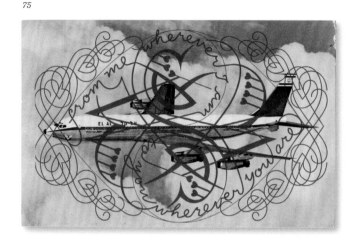

Anagrama's branding for Theurel & Thomas displays that same level of skill and a fresh approach to traditional signals for romance and love. [72, 73] Theurel & Thomas is the first patisserie in Mexico, specializing in French macarons. The white palette is central to the design to highlight the bright colors of the macarons. It also speaks to purity, weddings, and innocent delicacies. The eighteenth-century French interior recalls the romance of intrigue at Versailles. The combination tells the visitor that this is the place to purchase treats in the service of true romance.

Each year, Marian Bantjes designs a Valentine's card for friends and clients. They are coveted artifacts that create joy for the recipient. Bantjes explores the ideas of love in many forms. In 2018, Bantjes had cards stamped with a foil design over 300 vintage Harlequin Romance novel covers from the 1960s through the 1980s. The result is a remarkable comment on simplified popular portrayals of love with sentimental and expected imagery. The foil stamped intricate forms made of hearts challenge the viewer to see the "love"

through the chains or briars of the pattern. They also suggest a kind of imprisonment and stasis, with the lovelorn faces trapped behind the beautiful web. [74]

Previously, in 2012, Bantjes designed a series of Valentine's cards with postcards and an overprinting in silver, "From me wherever I am / To you wherever you are." Here, she explores the postcard as an artifact. [75] It represents a moment when one wished to communicate with family or friends, conveying love and the need for connection. A postcard carries little information. At most, it tells the recipient where the sender is and a few lines describing his or her experience. The object itself is what we recognize as the message. By appropriating used postcards and strangers' experiences, Bantjes reinforces the power of the object itself. The overprinted message is another layer of emotion, Bantjes's message of love to a new recipient.

In contrast, nineteenth-century Valentine's cards exhibit the benefits of industrialization and lithography. [76] These cards were elaborately decorated with open-work lace paper, colored paper, and imagery. The

elaborateness of the card proved the level of love for the intended recipient. The imagery celebrates an agrarian and simple existence. Urban life, with its complexities and contradictions, is rejected. The subjects in the cards live pleasant lives with only the purest of intentions. Children, Cupid, flowers, and birds adorn the cards with pastel tones and gold paper. The message here is about romantic love and attachment. Innocence and purity are the only acceptable messages. Here, there is no lust or anything dangerous, exotic, or mature.

The complexity of love presents a designer with a difficult task. The reward, however, is a deeper connection to the viewer. Recognizing the multiplicity of definitions and focusing on one with purpose creates the most meaningful exchanges. It is tempting to communicate love with a red heart or symbol of Cupid alone, but these state "love," with no intensity or personal meaning. Love is not easy in life or design.

75

76
Collection of valentine
and greeting cards
**Kate Greenaway,
Breitkopf & Härtel,
Ernest Nister, and
others**
1850–80

Chapter 4: Humor

As E. B. White stated, "Analyzing humor is like dissecting a frog. Few people are interested, and the frog dies of it." Decoding humor is a tedious business. Philosophers have attempted to determine what is humorous and why for millennia. In the *Republic* (375 BCE), Plato recommended that the leadership of the state should refrain from laughter, "For ordinarily when one abandons himself to violent laughter, his condition provokes a violent reaction." Freud analyzed humor's properties and suggested that repression and sexuality caused it. Regardless of why we find something humorous, it is an extraordinary tool for the designer.

77

78

First, a designer can get away with more if the message or experience is humorous. One commonality with most jokes, witticisms, and puns is the element of surprise. For example, here is a joke by the comedian Henny Youngman: "While playing golf today, I hit two good balls. I stepped on a rake." This joke works because it walks us down an expected path, "While playing golf today…" and it provides action, "I hit two good balls." The surprise is the action of stepping on a rake. The audience needs to imagine the scene visually to understand precisely which balls Youngman is describing. The surprise has a slightly off-color tone. We enjoy the unforeseen, the collision of our expectations, and the mental process.

People enjoy solving problems. It is inherent. We solve a problem and receive a rush of chemicals in our brain that produces a pleasant sensation. Humor asks us to solve a problem, then provides an answer in a way we did not anticipate. Comedy also invites us to be "bad." Consider the typical heroic narrative, Odysseus in *The Odyssey* or Luke Skywalker in *Star Wars*. Heroic warrior characters follow the most virtuous ideals.

In contrast, Han Solo is funny. He recognizes a practical reality and an appreciation for more human activities such as drinking, eating, fighting, sleeping, and sex. He would subscribe to the wise Irish proverb: "It is better to be a coward for a minute than dead for the rest of your life."

In *Comic Relief: A Comprehensive Philosophy of Humor*, John Morreall provides the example of humor as a tool to accept negative information. An example is this debt-collection letter:

> We appreciate your business but, please, give us a break. Your account is overdue for ten months. That means we've carried you longer than your mother did.

When a designer faces the task of communicating a complex, socially controversial, or unpopular message, he or she uses humor as a gateway into the message.

For several years the performing and visual arts festival La Bâtie, in Geneva, commissioned Neo Neo to design all of its marketing materials. [77] The Neo Neo team created a mantra to follow: "We always try to communicate with an offbeat, absurd tone using images that you would not usually use to promote cultural events."

The 2017 festival's graphics comment on social media, selfies, and personal identity politics. This range of content might be dense, dark, and forbidding. This is not a typically smart approach to attract visitors.

In contrast, Neo Neo worked with rounded letterforms, and a light pink background reinforces the lightness of the event. [78] They added smiley faces in various forms that might relate to bliss, a rave, or more licentious emotions. Using the smiley emoji to create a halftone pattern for the images provides a moment of surprise and discovery for the viewer. The audience is not repulsed by the voyeuristic images but is pleased with the humor. [79]

Iconography and visual tone provide quick visual cues to the audience. We see the bright color and happy symbols and are reassured that the message is positive. For example, when artist Jeremy Deller and graphic design studio Fraser Muggeridge created an identity system for Somerset House's 2016 season, they began with a five-hundred-year-old text. Thomas More published *Utopia* in 1516, a novel about a fictional island society. More also created a Utopian alphabet.

79

77–79
Posters and
publications for
La Bâtie Festival
**Thuy-An Hoang,
Xavier Erni**
at Neo Neo
2017

80

81

82

83

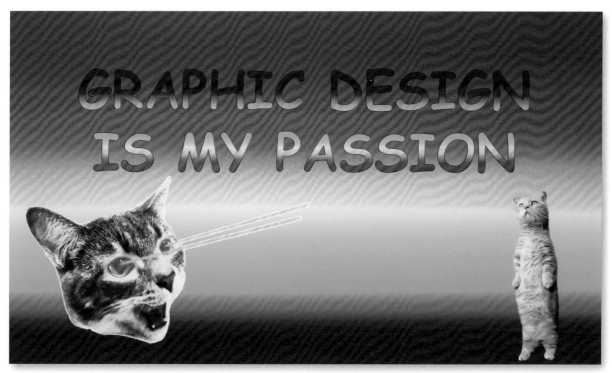

84

85

86
Campaign button
for 1968 Republican
Presidential candidate
Richard Nixon
unknown
1968

87
Poster for the film
Love in the Afternoon
Saul Bass
1957

86

Deller and Fraser Muggeridge based their work on this alphabet, transforming it into twenty-first-century idioms, relating to rave culture and social media, stating, "It's a great image that a caveman would understand, associated with all kind of utopias: consumer, religious, and youth culture." [80]

Of course, there will always be curmudgeons who insist that design is serious, and there is no room for frivolity. Yes, design is a serious business, but levity provides joy. At times, there may be no deep and meaningful message. Laughter can exist, like art, for its own sake. A happy flower in a flower pot may not contain multiple levels of meaning, but it is disarming. [81]

Asking the viewer to recognize a symbol provides a layer of intimacy. I will feel good when I spend time examining a puzzle and then solving it. For a series of characters on a promotion for fonts.com I used letterforms to create individuals rather than highlighting the typeface, Didoni, with an alphabet. I named the characters for added personality: Earl, Velma, Montgomery, Mr. James, and Eudora. [82]

If humor connects to the immoral or "naughty," Angad Singh's poster, *Graphic Design is My Passion*, succeeds for a design audience. [83] Comic Sans, cat heads, and a hackneyed gradient are all forbidden in the world of "good design." The result is a humorous combination of images that exaggerates the forbidden. Beneath the veneer of comedy, the poster asks questions about memes as language, the reiteration of culture, and the depersonalization of design with ubiquitous digital tools.

For the 2015 La Bâtie festival, Neo Neo appropriated the visual language of fast food graphics and mascots. [84] The design team applied the friendly and juvenile characters to media across Geneva. The design asks the audience to recognize one message, fast-food restaurant communication, and then reinterpret that message for an arts festival.

Ian Lynam worked with the concept of misdirection on the cover for *Slanted* magazine in Tokyo. The viewer expects the cover of one of the most popular international graphic design magazines to feature serious graphic design, or at the least, a minimal symbolic pun. But Lynam uses

Japanese typography and a curve on a pink background. The message, told with a wink, is the vibrance and excitement of graphic design in Tokyo. [85] Like the fonts.com characters as a substitute for the expected alphabet sample, the disconnect is the trigger for humor. The audience attempts to understand and deconstruct the image and is rewarded with something amusing.

A clever double entendre, written or visual, drags the viewer into the design. At first, the viewer may be shocked that a vulgar message is publicly displayed. The viewer feels relief, and is simultaneously entertained upon the recognition that there is another meaning. A double entendre is a powerful tool with which to create a personal, and subsequently, memorable message.

An off-color slogan on a button for the 1968 Republican National Convention is, at first glance, shocking, but actually refers to presidential candidate Richard "Dick" Nixon. [86] And, of course, closing the shade is the first step one takes when having an affair in the afternoon. [87]

87

89

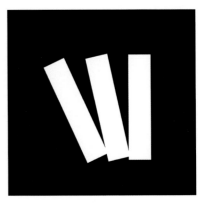

88

Similarly, well-placed humor elevates a mundane process to the memorable. Paula Scher's signage for a New York parking garage asks the obvious question on the building's Scrabble-like window pattern. {88} The typography tells the viewer, "This parking garage is friendlier than the others down the street." Humor becomes a unique selling proposition while adding a moment of delight in the tedious process of finding a parking spot.

Anton Tielemans's logo for the Wentworth County Libraries System is another remarkable example of the power to command the reader's attention by mixing language systems. {89} What appears first as three books on a shelf is then recognized as a *W*. This is an unusually successful application of camouflage. Once the observer sees the *W* and the books, he or she can never see one without the other. The joy and emotional experience in deciphering the image/letter provide mnemonic value.

A direct and honest announcement in an unexpected setting creates unease in the messenger's receiver. {90} Milton Glaser and Seymour Chwast challenged the audience's

90

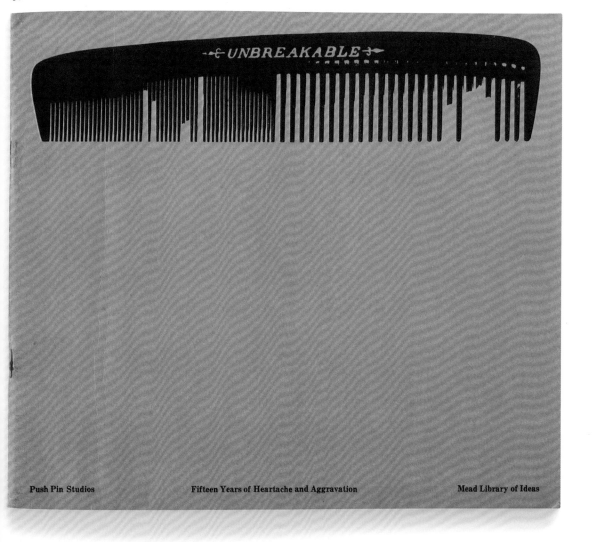

Push Pin Studios   Fifteen Years of Heartache and Aggravation   Mead Library of Ideas

91
Don Alonso de Suquía
book cover and back
Pràctica
2017

92
H.L. Mencken
Speaking album cover
Matthew Liebowitz
1960

93
Illustration in the
Party Tricks chapter
of *Esquire's Handbook*
for Hosts
L. J. Allen
1949

91

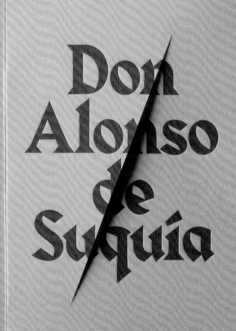

92

93

...AND DIRTY TRICKS

expectation of a positive message on a poster for their firm, Push Pin Studios: "Fifteen years of Heartache and Aggravation." The audience is forced to reconcile the dramatic statement with the expectation of a typical and upbeat anniversary message. The unbreakable comb provides comic relief. The image is a visual pun, reassuring the viewer that the message is hopeful rather than cynical.

Don Alonso de Suquía is a novella that follows the adventures of swordsman Don Alonso de Suquía after the reconquest of Granada in 1491. Carlos Bermudez, Albert Porta, and Guillem Casasus's cover logically pairs medieval Spanish typography with Spain's national colors, red and yellow. {91} The die-cut slash interrupts the reading, suggesting a dramatic swordsman in the vein of El Cid or Juana Garcia de Arintero. A traditional leather-bound book cover with symmetrical classical typography communicates earnest and humorless content. This cover, however, relies on action, energy, and entertainment, reassuring us that the reading of this book is not a dull and solemn task.

Designers are in the business of verbal and visual language; therefore, it is not surprising that a standard design tactic is subverting or amplifying our perception of language. In 1960, Matthew Liebowitz applied quotation marks around the image of the controversial satirist, Henry Louis Mencken. {92} The viewer must reconcile two methods of reading. First, he or she reads the letterforms as expected, to understand the information. Second, the viewer is interrupted by the image of Mencken and asked to adjust to visual, image-based reading. The result is a sense of pleasure in deciphering the puzzle.

Humor provides us with an avenue to imagine life outside of acceptable social standards. Jokes succeed when they venture into territory that makes us uncomfortable. Stress and humor work together. A comedian suggests a scenario that is either extremely personal or controversial. The punchline allows the audience to exhale and laugh. Serene humor often fails. It isn't a good idea to pull a chair out from under a guest at a dinner party. However, in a comedy, it is seen as slapstick (still not a good idea). {93}

94

The reinvention of the ordinary asks us to rethink what we expect. Taiwanese designer Guan-Hao Pan tackled the issue of determining the correct condom size with packaging design. Condoms are classically only four sizes: small, medium, large, and extra-large, with girth being more important to the correct fit of the condom than length. Also, men notoriously, overestimate the size required, leading to the wrong choice and risk of slippage. Pan addressed the issue with an ingenious and humorous solution based on vegetables—the Love Guide Condoms.

Determining whether one's size is a banana or carrot minimizes the self-image concerns with labels "small" and "extra-large." The system is also understandable to anyone, man or woman, who has held a vegetable or ... The elegant packaging has none of the standard trappings of ultra-masculine condom packaging such as black glossy foil with machine style typography and rivets. The bright colors and straightforward typography appear easy to understand and innocuous enough for anyone to purchase without embarrassment. {94, 95}

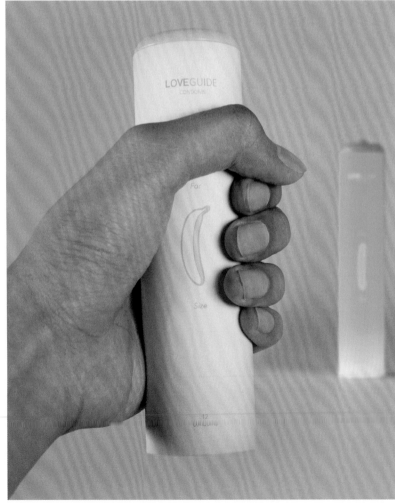

95

94
Love Guide Condoms
packaging
**Guan-Hao Pan and
Meng-Cong Zheng**
2015

95
Love Guide Condoms
container for
individual condoms

96

96
AIGA Humor Show
poster
**Alexander Isley and
Tibor Kalman**
1986

97
Bal du Cinéma poster
Raymond Savignac
1953

97

This approach, a visual puzzle that requires a solution, is especially potent when targeted precisely. Raymond Savignac's poster depicting a heroic leading man on the screen who needs a little lift is targeted at cinema aficianados. {97}

For an exhibition of humorous graphic design by AIGA, Tibor Kalman and Alex Isley looked to one of the artifacts of a graphic designer's professional life, a printer's press sheet. {96} Print designers recognize the color bars, crop marks, and written notations. The recipient of the poster reads it as follows here:

» This is a press sheet. I recognize it.
» It is part of my world.
» It is trimmed incorrectly. The color bars are in the center, and the image is offset from the center.
» Something happened.
» Oh, yes, it's a banana. People slip on banana peels in comedies.
» The printer slipped and trimmed this badly.
» And it's for a humor exhibition.
» That's funny.

This simple path follows the classic structure of a joke: first, provide the recognizable setting, next, throw in a conflict, and finally end with an answer that is unexpected yet entirely logical.

The reinvention of the ordinary asks us to rethink what we expect. We recognize a wine cork. It is a cylinder made of cork material that holds the wine in the bottle. When we are presented with an image of a wine cork that does not match our expectations, we need to rethink our understanding and understand the new image. When the cork becomes a face, we find an object we can recognize. When it then adopts the characteristic of regional identity, we find added satisfaction in recognizing the message, wines of the world, with each character representing the wine's origin. Three levels of frustration and relief are exhibited here. With each step of entertaining problem solving, the observer feels increasingly more intelligent and, therefore, connected to the product. {98}

98

826 Valencia assists students in under-
served communities with writing skills.
Founders, educator Nínive Calegari and
author Dave Eggers, found a space for the
organization in San Francisco. Unfortunately, the city had zoned it as strictly a
retail space. Realizing that there is a lack of
pirate supplies in the world, they opened a
pirate store in front of the writing lab.

The store sells supplies that pirates might
require: hooks, jailer keys, temporary
tattoos, eye patches, and other pirate
paraphernalia. The agency Office designed
the packaging and environment to support
the Pirate Supply Store. {99} The playful
and comedic nature of the things you can
buy there allows us to seriously consider
purchasing items typically used in pillaging
and sea battles. When we imagine using the
Peg Leg Oil, we move away from our daily
life of working, making dinner, and
commuting, into a safe adventure. This
creates an emotional bond that most brands
spend millions of dollars and many years
trying to forge.

The ability to suspend disbelief and accept
the ridiculous is part of the process in
comedy. Taken literally, or without humor,
the ridiculous often simply seems stupid.

98
Wines of the World
packaging
**Nacho Lavernia and
Alberto Cinefuegas at
Lavernia Cinefuegas**
2012

99
Packaging for
826 Valencia
Tenderloin Center
**Office: Jason Schulte
Design**
2015

99

100

100
Branding system for
Mexico Restaurante
y Barre
**Sean Adams at
AdamsMorioka**
2006

Designing for a restaurant is an exciting prospect. The designer helps to create an environment and message for people to enjoy. But there are financial challenges in the materials required to operate, beyond food and staff. A restaurant may need a hundred menus, and they need to resist oily hands while not feeling "cheap." There are a multitude of items that quickly escalate the costs: take-out menus and packaging, bags, placemats, postcards, signage, dinnerware, and uniforms.

In the mid-2000s, at the height of the recession, the noted chef Larry Nicola asked AdamsMorioka to design a new Mexican restaurant with a limited budget. Rather than working against the low budget limitations, we embraced them. I adopted the mantra, "Quality is Job 2." Analog tools such as hand-painting and a typewriter replaced any high-end and refined digital production. When the creative team experienced trepidation about designing "cheap" we created a fictional designer who had limited talent and skill but enormous enthusiasm.

This concocted person designed everything with energy and excitement, ignoring most rules of color, layout, and production. The placemats vibrated with the wrong combination of blue and red. We applied bad photographs from a recent trip to Mexico City to the postcards. We sourced vinyl menus in a color not used since 1974 from a company in Arizona and painted the building in a bright pink that could not be ignored. The overstatement of the concept, exceeding any bounds of good taste, added the humor and set the tone for the restaurant. {100}

Humor can successfully motivate, convince, or persuade an audience. Intelligence and respect for the audience are the commonalities shared by the best examples. These do not underestimate the viewer's ability to make sense of the message. Humor disarms and then speaks to the viewer and forms a personal, positive, and emotional connection.

Chapter 5: Intelligence

Designers convey intelligence with a variety of means: technical forms, geometric or documentary-type images, hard shapes, and multiple entry points to the information or operation of a designed artifact. In design, intelligence is the opposite of innocence, presuming a deeper understanding of the world, complexity, and contradictions. Intelligence has many meanings. It refers to the ability to solve problems, intellectual aptitude, machine learning, and national defense. In this context, we will focus on design that communicates intelligence as solving problems and intellectual aptitude.

101

**Massachusetts
Institute
of Technology**

**Woods Hole
Oceanographic
Institution**

**Joint Program
Graduate Study**

**Physical
Oceanography**

**Marine
Geophysics**

Marine Geology

**Chemical
Oceanography**

Nature of the program

This is a program of graduate study
in oceanography conducted jointly by
the two institutions and leading to the
doctorate awarded jointly by the two
institutions. It covers many aspects
of physical, chemical, geophysical
and geological oceanography.
Course work is done both at M.I.T.
in Cambridge and at W.H.O.I. in
Woods Hole. Thesis work may be
done at either institution, as may be
appropriate in a given case.

Students in this program have the
advantage of the combined
resources of faculty and facilities
of a major university and of the many
scientists and faculty and special
facilities, including ships, of a world-
renowned oceanographic institution.

Admission

Admission is competitive as judged
by representatives of the two institutions. It is based on the extent and
quality of the applicant's previous
academic work, particularly in the
physical sciences and mathematics.
No previous academic preparation
in oceanography is required. However, some background in the earth
sciences is desirable for students
planning to specialize in marine
geology.

Financial aid

Fellowships, traineeships, teaching
and research assistantships are
available on a competitive basis each
year to entering or continuing students. All of these forms of financial
aid cover tuition plus a modest
stipend toward living expenses.

For further information, address

Professor Henry G. Houghton, Head
Department of Meteorology
Massachusetts Institute of
Technology
Cambridge, Massachusetts 02139
or
Professor Frank Press, Head
Department of Geology and
Geophysics
Massachusetts Institute of
Technology
Cambridge, Massachusetts 02139
or
Dr. H. Burr Steinbach
Dean of Graduate Studies
Woods Hole Oceanographic
Institution
Woods Hole, Massachusetts 02543

101
MIT Woods Hole
Oceanographic
Institution poster
Dietmar Winkler
1967

102
COBOL publication
**United States
Department of
Defense**
1960

103
COBOL poster
Dietmar Winkler
1969

102

Certain items demand the appearance of intelligence, such as a medical textbook or poster for an avant-garde music festival. And certain people prefer to be considered smart. Intelligence in design does not exclude affirmative behavioral requirements: usability, clear function, and a recognizable form. An item that is impossible to operate or understand may appear intellectually challenging but will fail to engage the user.

In design, intelligence is the opposite of innocence, presuming a deeper understanding of the world, complexity, and contradictions. The goal of the designer is to quickly state to the viewer, "This is intellectual and rational," as opposed to a message of innocence that relies on naivety and minimal information.

Let's begin with some of the expectations we have when confronting a message or product that is intelligent and mature.
» Dense information.
» Devoid of emotion and sentimentality.
» Sharp forms and geometry.
» Rational typography.
» Multiple entry points for understanding complex information.

Marvin Minsky, a cofounder of the Massachusetts Institute of Technology's AI laboratory, explored necessary ingredients essential to all intelligence in his paper, "Communication with Alien Intelligence."
» Subgoals: break hard problems into simpler ones.
» Sub-Objects: make descriptions based on parts and relations.
» Cause-Symbols: explain and understand how things change.
» Memories: accumulate experience about similar problems.
» Economics: efficiently allocate scarce resources.
» Planning: organize work before filling in details.
» Self-Awareness: provide for the problem-solvers' own welfare.

These attributes are fundamental in design to communicate a profound message. The MIT Office of Design Services from the 1960s through the 1980s and its designers Jacqueline Casey, Muriel Cooper, Ralph Coburn, and Dietmar Winkler was one of the United States' most innovative design groups. The designers managed complex information and technical discourse that was visually groundbreaking. They combined the International Swiss Style,

mathematics, grids, and precision, with dynamic forms and colors. This remarkable group of designers worked with geometric rigor, but unlike lifeless examples of other International Style design, added a bold vitality to their work. {101}

In comparison to the United States' Department of Defense COBOL manual, {102} we can deconstruct Dietmar Winkler's poster for a COBOL programming course at MIT, applying Minsky's ingredients for (alien) intelligence. {103}

Winkler communicates the complexities of COBOL with inviting simplicity (Subgoals). He uses geometric forms to create a puzzle for the viewer to solve (Sub-Objects). The circular forms build from individual elements to create the title, as COBOL does in a programming language (Cause-Symbols). The puzzle relies on the viewer's experience with geometry, understanding how the forms relate (Memories). Winkler separates the information with a clear hierarchy with an emphasis on minimal typography (Economics, Planning). Finally, the holistic experience of the poster is engaging and the viewer's experience pleasurable (Self-Awareness).

103

Lowell Institute School
under the auspices of the
Massachusetts Institute of
Technology

Special Summer
Computer Course
Introduction to
COBOL Programming

Description
A special summer computer
course supported by M.I.T.'s
Project MAC to introduce
students to COBOL programming, that is, writing and
interpreting COBOL-type programs. Students who take the
course will be exposed to
most facets of COBOL pro-
gramming — a good founda-
tion for job advancement.
(No placement services are
provided.)

Requirements
Completion of high school or
its equivalent. No mathematics is required beyond high
school algebra. No programming experience is nec-
essary. Students will be
selected from the list of
applicants. Because of facilities, class size will be
limited to 75.

The Course
Ten weeks beginning
June 30, 1969.
Two classes each week:
Monday and Wednesday,
7-10. Computer time will be
available.
Two examinations.
Ten quizzes (one each week).
Three or four programs (one
every two to three weeks).
Six other homework
assignments.

Cost
$5 tuition.
$10 computer time.

Information
Lowell Institute School
UN 4-6900, extension 4895
Charles Kidwell 864-3564.

Deadline
Applications must be
received before June 25.
Notification of acceptance
will be mailed shortly there-
after. No course outline is
available at this time.

104
Rautenstrauch-
Joest-Museum:
Death and the Afterlife
exhibition
Atelier Brückner
2010
Photographer:
Michael Jungblut

As conscious human beings, we are
self-aware. Our brains can recognize its
operation, and we can conceptualize
experiences beyond our own. Communication on the reflective level, connected to
identity, culture, beliefs, and self-image, is
persuasive. Designing for a response on the
reflective level demands clear and intelligent delivery. Consider Atelier Brückner's
design for a section of *Death and the
Afterlife,* an exhibition at Rautestrauch-
Joest-Museum. This subject cannot pander
to our visceral response. {104}

Nobody would visit. Ever. Atelier Brückner
deftly manages to present issues regarding
death and belief with a combination of
objective information paired with no overt
religious bias.

The designers bathed this section in white,
a traditional color for death in many
cultures. They placed artifacts to allow the
visitor to discover the information in parts,
eventually defining his or her point of view.
Interactive elements engage the visitor,
allowing for additional moments of
personal discovery. The rational yet
emotionally charged design solution
succeeds with its sparse and mathematically precise environment in contrast to the

106

105

105
Au Sud d'Aujourd'hui
identity program
**Lizá Defossez
Ramalho and
Artur Rebelo at R2**
2015

106
IBM Pavillon,
New York World's Fair
**Charles and
Ray Eames and
Eero Saarinen**
1964

107
AIGA Design
Conference 2017
program
Sean Adams
Photographer:
Blake Little
2017

107

handmade cultural elements. The visitor's
experience is learning, not being indoctri-
nated in any one religion.

The puzzle is typical in design focused on
intelligence or an intellectual audience.
IBM's exhibition for the 1964 New York
World's Fair was a giant egg. {106} The
theater inside raised the audience into the
oval form. Charles and Ray Eames created a
presentation of images and film on multiple
screens. Each audience member interpreted the story differently as he or she
combined the images into one message.

The design firm R2 designed a visual
system for an exhibition of twelve Portuguese artists. The typography presents a
typographic puzzle mapping the
Portuguese contemporary artistic
creations. The designers based the forms
on cartography, displaying the cardinal
points (north, south, east, and west) and the
rectangular shape of Portugal. The team at
R2 positioned information relating to the
artists and work of the exhibition. {105}

To communicate the idea of connections for
the 2017 AIGA Design Conference, I chose
to avoid expected metaphors such as
handshaking. Instead, Blake Little

108

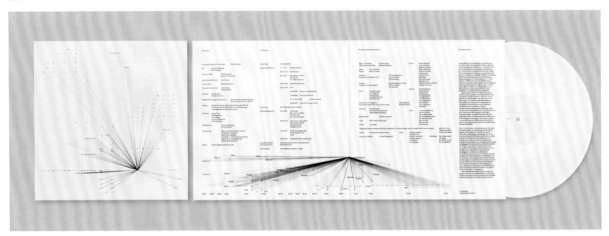

109

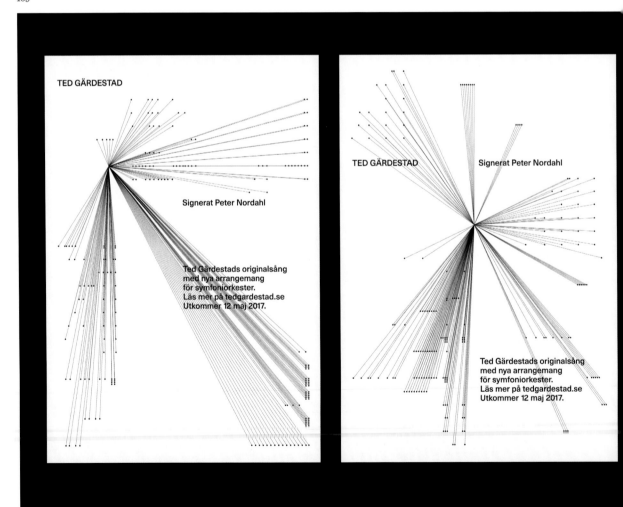

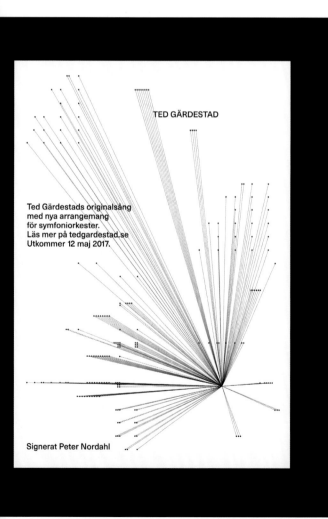

produced a collection of extreme close-ups of magnets. I applied the images, such as a cluster of magnetic slivers, to all materials, but did not explain why. The visual system is minimal. It rejects the chaos and graphic-heavy solutions common at the time, in favor of simple information design. This allowed the magnet images to be a priority visually, forcing the viewer to question and then recognize the image. [107]

In addition to asking the viewer to solve a puzzle, design with intelligence as an attribute will provide multiple entry points. Intelligent design may also apply precise geometry and three-dimensional layers to convey the complexity of the content. Stockholm Design Lab's album design for a remastering of Ted Gärdestad's music includes these elements. [108] Gärdestad is one of Sweden's most acclaimed recording artists. His work was a remarkable combination of multiple musical styles: Scandinavian acoustic, jazz, rock and roll, country, and others. Although he passed away in 1997, his music has seen an enormous revival in Sweden. Stockholm Design Lab's work for albums, posters, motion, and interactive design incorporates the concepts of collaboration, musical variety, and layers of meaning. [109]

110
IBM Selectric
typewriter
Eliot Noyes
1961

111
Vakuum publication
Marion Dönneweg
2017

110

In contrast, the IBM Selectric typewriter, designed by Eliot Noyes, is a smooth and straightforward form. {110} The Selectric introduced a ball mechanism, replacing the mechanical carriage return system. This provided the option of changing typefaces by choosing another ball.

Noyes designed the typewriter with clay models typical of automobile design. "We tried to emphasize the singleness and simpleness of form," Noyes explained, "by making the whole shape something like that of a stone so that you are aware of the continuity of the sides and under the machine and over the top." The keys on the IBM Selectric are closer to ovals than the traditional circle. Each key is slightly depressed in the center to accommodate the finger's shape.

The Selectric owned 75 percent of the market by 1986. It was the first step toward desktop publishing, foreshadowing the attention to design adopted by Apple twenty years later. The shift from complex and mechanical to biomorphic and minimalist industrial design for technology is profound. We now expect friendly simplicity

from the intelligent products that we operate. A desktop computer with complex forms would be charming and retro, but not expected to be high technology.

Marion Dönneweg's identity system for Vakuum adopts a comparable tone, applying simplicity of form to a complex concept. {111} Vakuum is a consultancy and laboratory for gastronomic research, development, and processes founded by Martin Lippo, one of Spain's leading chefs. Dönneweg describes the concept: "Vakuum is emptiness. It is the absence, the beginning, and a blank mind. Vakuum is weightless, a place to be suspended, space which is governed by other laws." The lab is a space where innovation allows for anything to happen.

The visuals are disarmingly simple. A shape similar to the Selectric keys sits on a single image or alone in a white expanse. Dönneweg's typography is sublime. She applied a simple and bold sans serif to minimal text with nothing extraneous.

Dönneweg asks the viewer to decipher the meaning of the image paired with, shape, and text with no overt description. The

result is a deeper connection to the message once the viewer recognizes the weightlessness in the image, text such as "Take a breath. Make your mind empty," and a shape that appears to be in flux between a circle and a square. Dönneweg frames the concept of nothingness in a manner that engages the viewer with intelligence and respect. She creates the existence and appearance of absence.

The twentieth-century television is an illustration of style over function. Until the early 2000s, when flat-screen displays became common, all television sets functioned in the same way. A Philco Predicta television operated with cathode ray tubes to display an image and play audio. {112} The RCA Victor Color television worked the same. To communicate differences and advances in technology, engineers and designers created different exterior styling for different audiences.

The Predicta might appeal to a family with its friendly shape and gravity-defying appearance. The Videosphere and TR 005 Orbitel promised a Jetsons-style future with an astronaut helmet or spaceship form and color. {113, 116}

111

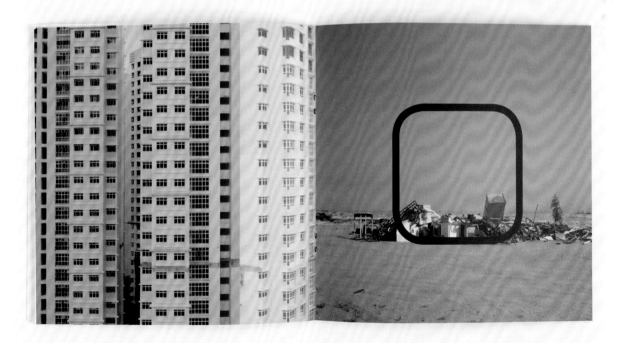

112

113

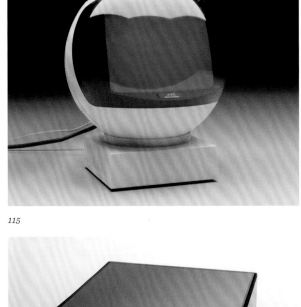

114

115

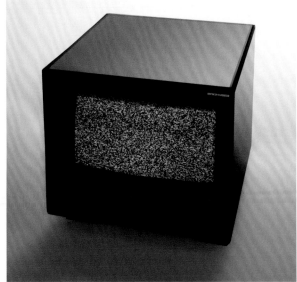

116

117

117
International
Design Conference
announcement
Louis Danziger
1955

118
Adopt-a-Book poster
Lucille Tenazas
1992

In Aspen 1955   June 13 to 18

INTERNATIONAL DESIGN CONFERENCE

Five thought-provoking days of Design talk with
many of the most distinguished thinkers from
all parts of the world.
For full details write to:
International Design Conference
220 South Michigan Avenue
Chicago 4, Illinois

And then there is the remarkably large and bulky console set, such as the RCA Mediterranean Sanlucar. [114] These consoles often included built-in record and eight-track players. RCA, Zenith, Magnavox, and other manufacturers designed these massive entertainment centers as trophy furniture. The Mediterranean, early American, and Chippendale styles surrounded the television screen to blend in with a family's living room or den.

The Brionvega television, however, is a sculpture. [115] Mario Bellini designed the television to appear as a simple black cube when turned off. The controls are not easy to see to maintain the purity of the cube. Bellini recognized the audience that preferred an intelligent and sophisticated object in a highly designed interior. While it may have a slick Darth Vader black exterior when turned off, the light from the screen glows from the inside, creating a luminous box.

The Brionvega is a perfect example that understatement is a tenet of design directed to an intellectual audience. An even more radical example of understatement is

Lou Danziger's announcement for the International Design Conference in Aspen in 1955. [117] The vast negative space, prized by designers, is about modernist ideas such as "less is more" and truth in materials. The invitation speaks to a narrow group of mid-century designers who considered themselves to be cultured and urbane. The simple and refined typography tells us that every choice here is purposeful and created with skill. A subtext here is that "the masses" might expect garish color and big typography, but a real designer appreciates the minimal intelligent solution.

Similarly, Lucille Tenazas's poster for an Adopt a Book program asks the viewer to create a narrative from a sepia image of a branch, stone, open book, and leaf. [118]

The overt directive is to attend the event and adopt a book. The covert message is about the importance of literacy, beauty of a book as an object, and quiet contemplation when reading. Tenazas's typography and visual forms play with transparency and three-dimensional space. Again, these are

signals that this is not a children's book event with bright colors and easy to access content. The understated elegance and color palette reinforces the intellectual nature of the event.

Designing to communicate intelligence straddles the line between purely rational and emotional. People prefer an easy option, regardless of intellectual capacity. A message presented in a manner that allows the receiver to process the information effortlessly creates a more pleasurable experience than the oblique message.

Hampton Dunlap's proposal for the 2028 Los Angeles Olympics walks that line. The information that the viewer needs to access, the schedule and location, is clear and direct. The opposite side of the poster follows the same structure of a grid and minimal typography choices. However, it adds an image and logo treatment that asks the viewer to solve the puzzle. Dunlap applies bright colors that honor the 1984 Los Angeles and the 1968 Mexico City Olympics. These add a positive aesthetic experience and an emotional connection to the content. [119]

118

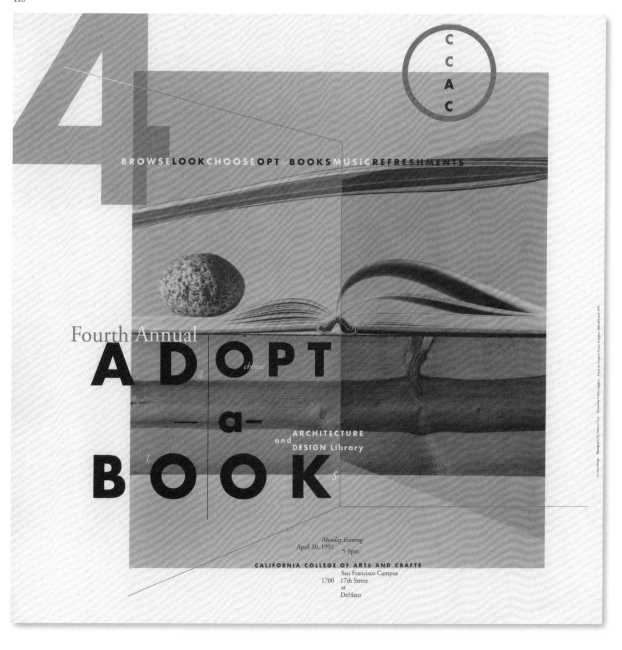

BROWSE LOOK CHOOSE OPT *for* BOOKS MUSIC REFRESHMENTS

Fourth Annual
ADOPT a BOOK

ARCHITECTURE and DESIGN Library

Monday Evening
April 20, 1992 5-9pm

CALIFORNIA COLLEGE OF ARTS AND CRAFTS
San Francisco Campus
1700 17th Street
at
DeHaro

119
LA Olympics 2028
campaign proposal
Hampton Dunlap
2019

120
Büro Uebele website
Büro Uebele
2020

121
The Babysitter poster
Michael Bierut
2000

119

122
Eames House
with Eames furniture
**Charles and
Ray Eames**
1950

123
Credenza 4 Position
Florence Knoll
1954

122

123

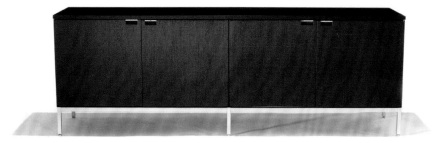

Many websites overlook access to information. If something can spin and twirl, it usually does. Büro Uebele's website, however, is refreshingly legible and accessible. The grid structure and use of just one size and color of the typeface, Verdana, provides a clear path for the viewer. The minimal approach solves two additional issues. First, the content on the site, Büro Uebele's work, is allowed to be the primary focus with no distracting twirling forms on the sidebar. Second, the International Style rigor communicates the firm's confidence, maturity, and intelligence.

It is the difference between a perfectly tailored black Armani suit that projects expertise and a flashy plaid suit that might look fun, but is rarely trustworthy and thoughtful. {120}

Michael Bierut's poster for *The Babysitter* displays the same minimal International Style, but with a surprise. The play, based on a short story by Robert Coover, is a series of vignettes dealing with sexual aggression, age, violence, infanticide, and adultery. This is difficult content. Beirut's objective visual tone steps away from judgment or bias. The facts are presented here in legible typogra-

phy. The only suggestion of sexual content is the phallic baby bottle. Again, the image is bare, black and white, and unattached to a hand or other body part. We do not know, as a symbolic image, what state of arousal or inability to perform, the bottle represents. The formal tone refuses to inform the audience that the play is a comedy, drama, or mystery. The intelligent voice asks the viewer to fill in the blanks. {121}

Lack of ornamentation and focus on function are cues that a product is efficient. Florence Knoll and Charles and Ray Eames dedicated their careers to efficiency and clarity. Their furniture design is reductive, rejecting any unnecessary element. The proportions and materials are flawless. Quality of construction is a hallmark with all of Knoll and the Eames's work. Now, here is the problem: how do we sell modern and straightforward furniture to a nation accustomed to heavily cushioned sofas and ornamental woodwork on cabinetry?

Knoll produced and sold Florence Knoll's work. {123} Herman Miller worked with Charles and Ray Eames. {122} Both compa-

nies marketed the furniture, not to average buyers seeking a comfortable chair regardless of style, but to an intellectual and cultural elite. These individuals visited museums, worked in creative fields, and looked for the new and exciting.

For the general public, modernism and modern art in the 1950s represented the urbane and intellectual. A pipe-smoking professor must own an Eames Lounge chair. The modern woman insisted on a Knoll credenza for the house. Mid-century modernism continues to be a symbol of an educated and cultivated consumer. And of European villains in movies. They always have modern furniture.

There are contradictions to the rules of efficiency and ease of use. The impenetrable espresso machine conveys an appreciation for the best coffee. The owner must be an aficionado of the best, and bright enough to operate the machine. More spouts and knobs clearly state, "I am serious about coffee." In contrast, the unassuming Mr. Coffee or an antique coffee pot with a straightforward operation is charming, but far from perspicacious.

Chapter 6: Elegance

Let's revisit Donald Norman's levels of response to design: visceral, behavioral, and reflective. Of these, reflective design is the most fluid and powerful response. The reflective level is about conscious thought, not a biological or behavioral reaction. It is based on cultural learning, individual experience, belief systems, and values. One can have a visceral response to a grotesque painting, but the reflective can intellectually override the feeling and determine that it is remarkably elegant. One culture may esteem honest and straightforward design, while another may regard it as dull.

124

124
Classic Century
Collection dinnerware
Eva Zeisel
1955

125
Potpourri vase
(pot-pourri à vaisseau)
Sèvres Manufactory
1757–58

126
Wall Clock (Pendule)
**possibly after a
design by Juste-
Aurèle Meissonnier**
1735–1740

125

Our self-identity is represented in the reflective. Everybody can understand the experience of going to school in an embarrassing outfit considered fantastic by a grandmother. We can feel shame for wearing sneakers purchased at a discount department store while others wear new Nike or Adidas shoes. This connects to the socioeconomic value we ascribe to a product. Prestige, uniqueness, and expense work at the reflective level. The owner of an elaborate gilded clock places it in a prominent location to be viewed by guests. It is the rarity and cost of the clock that provides reflective value. [126] The same clock mass-produced in plastic and sold at Ikea may be just as beautiful but is far less impressive to a guest.

A common misperception is that design is Darwinian in the sense that it is improves over time. Design is indeed Darwinian, but in terms of actual evolution, it is a product of its time and place. What we value today aesthetically and culturally is a product of our history and experience. A Sèvres vase produced in 1757 is no less incredible than a twentieth-century Eva Zeisel collection of porcelain. Only wealthy individuals could afford porcelain in the eighteenth century. The French aristocracy prized Sèvres

porcelain with hand-painted scenes and little practical use. To own something this delicate, ornate, and useless was a sign of real wealth. [125]

After World War II, consumers valued simplicity, beauty, and ease of use. People wanted graceful objects that could be used daily. In 1955, Eva Zeisel created a line of pottery for Hall China, the Century Collection. The collection provided precisely what the post-war consumer wanted: elegance and utility. She designed with organic shapes, a common theme after the chaos and destruction of World War II. The pottery is delicate and sensuous but can manage gravy in the gravy bowl without cracking and stand up to washing. A fan of Zeisel's work might consider the Sèvres vase as ornate and useless. The opposite is also true. A French aristocrat in 1757 might view the Century Collection as something for the staff too plebeian for decoration. [124]

The same parallel can be made with the book as an artifact. The *Shah Jahan Album* (1630–40) is no less amazing than a modern book. [127] As previously discussed, in the twenty-first century we appreciate efficiency, intelligence, and modesty of

126

127
*Rosette Bearing the
Name and Title of
Emperor Aurangzeb*
(Recto), from the *Shah
Jahan Album* book
Mir 'Ali Haravi
1630–40

128
*A Lesson with A.G.
Fronzoni* (*A Lezione con
A.G. Fronzoni*) book
**Daniele De Batté
and Davide Sossi at
Artiva Design**
2017

127

means. Artiva Design honored these values
with *A Lezione con A.G. Fronzoni* (*A Lesson
with A.G. Fronzoni*). [128] The book
embodies a design aesthetic vastly different
than the exquisite *Shah Jahan Album*.
Sophisticated typography, the graceful
square proportion, and deep black color
create a unified and pure solution. The
design reflects Fronzoni's values, "A
message, whatever it is, should be sincere,
appropriate, and essential."

The evolution from ornamentation to pure
function is not simple. Like all design
approaches, one solution shifts the norm
slightly, then another, and finally, the
majority respects simplicity and function
over ornament. Louis Sullivan, one of
America's most celebrated architects, sits
uncomfortably in between. Sullivan is
regarded as one of the first modernist
architects. He designed buildings that
served as the model for American skyscrap-
ers. [130] But, at the height of the
International Style in the 1960s, architectural critics dismissed Sullivan. His
beautiful pattern work was anathema to
"correct" modernist theory.

128

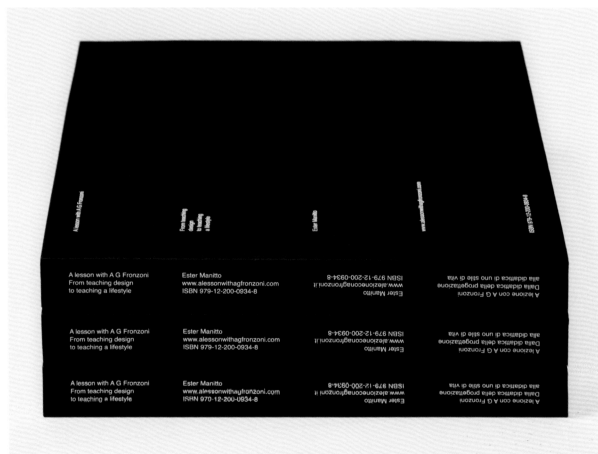

130

129

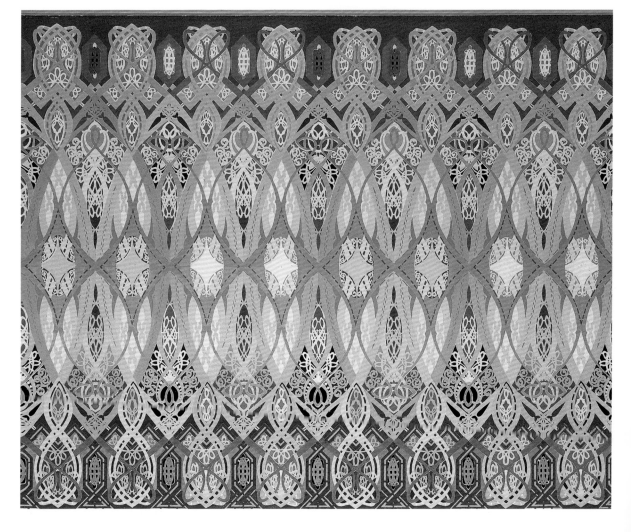

129
Chicago Stock
Exchange Trading
Room surface stencil
Louis H. Sullivan
1893

130
Wainright Building
**Adler, Sullivan, and
Ramsey, Architects**
1891

131
Princesse de Broglie
painting
**Jean-Auguste-
Dominique Ingres**
1851

and
Louis XIII style
Ovolo frame
unknown
c. 1958

131

Sullivan's ornamentation and pattern, based on natural forms, integrated, elegant styles into the building's structure. The wall stencil for the Chicago Stock Exchange trading room is a masterpiece of pattern with interwoven elements that played with the light in the room. {129}

In modernist theory, ornamentation should not exist in our world. But human beings are attracted to beauty, and a bare wall is, in time, only an empty wall. The ornate frame for Jean-Auguste-Dominique Ingres's painting of Princesse de Broglie is based on a Louis XIII form. {131} The mannerist forms include gilded flowers and vines, like Sullivan's ornament, with high levels of detail. This style of frame represented the height of sophistication in the nineteenth century. Today, one might regard it as busy or old-fashioned. Regardless of the style du jour, we viscerally respond to beautiful forms, but we make a conscious judgment on the reflective level.

In the "Seduction" and "Efficiency" chapters, we explored the golden section as a pleasing proportion. Applying other proportional systems adds to the perception of elegance. Human beings are good at

132

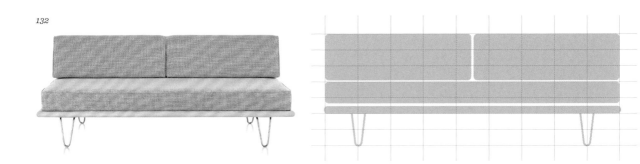

133

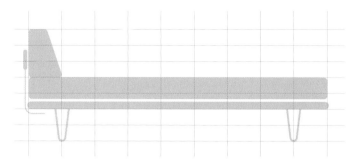

132
Nelson Daybed
George Nelson
1950

133
Vignette furniture
collection
Michael Vanderbyl
2010

creating order from chaos visually. We naturally arrange elements into groups. We look for consistencies and inconsistencies in form. When a designer works with a consistent proportion, we may not consciously recognize it. Few people look at a George Nelson Daybed and see a consistent ratio repeated and grid structure. Nevertheless, it is that order that provides the sense of elegance. {132}

Understandably, it is the more straightforward proportions and shapes that appeal to us. Complex forms ask us to make decisions, whereas a circle or square is easy to recognize. Michael Vanderbyl's furniture line, Vignette, religiously adheres to a strict and uncomplicated geometric system. He works with circular forms for the surface and base of the tables and chairs. The chairs are half circles within a cube. {133}

Like the Nelson Daybed, every form works with a strict geometric grid to maintain consistency. Vanderbyl designed the furniture ergonomically to fit a human body comfortably. The textiles are luxurious and minimal. These cues work together to create a holistic sense of functional harmony and elegance.

Scarcity and uniqueness add value economically and aesthetically. One appraises a rare object or one-of-a-kind as valuable. We consider an item to be elegant because we understand its high value. Our experiences and memories inform our judgment. A refined letterform with flawless curves is pleasing, and we ascribe aesthetic esteem as we recognize the rare talent to create it. {134} The Spencerian curves of the handmade typographic composition on a 1962 AIGA Award interweave in a way that a typeface can not replicate. {135} The award has value as an artifact representing expertise. The rarity of the item adds to its allure.

A well-made grid structure on a page or screen adds stability and grace to a project. The grid is often apparent with asymmetrical design with multiple columns, such as this book, and less visible in symmetrical layouts. Asymmetry signals modernity and efficiency in layout. The hierarchy of information is simpler to access, and multiple columns allow for flexibility. Symmetry reads as classical and elegant due to its long-established history. Within this context, designers follow ideal ratios that also signify harmony to the reader.

134

134
Pistilli Roman
typeface
**John Pistilli and
Herb Lubalin**
1964

135
AIGA Award
George Tscherny
1962

As early as the fifteenth century, printers utilized a consistent set of proportions for page layout. The outside column is wide, allowing room for written notations or the reader's thumb. The text area is scaled proportionately to accommodate between fifty to seventy characters, optimal for reading. To reinforce the traditional and elegant aesthetic, designers will typically use a classical serif typeface, such as Garamond, Caslon, or a modern interpretation, Sabon (Jan Tschichold, 1964). The typography is also scaled proportionately to create harmony. For example, a headline is set at twenty-four point, and the body text is typeset with eight-point type. {136–39}

Elegance is a device designers use to increase value, communicate the importance, and elevate a message for prestige. In our brains, when we see beauty, a large portion of the medial orbitofrontal cortex is activated. This is the same area that is connected to our emotions, decision-making, and feelings of pleasure. When we link a product, object, idea, or brand with elegance, we make an emotional, personal connection, and, subsequently, positive mnemonic association.

135

*Certificate
of Excellence from
The American Institute
of Graphic Arts
Design and Printing
for Commerce
1962*

Alvin Eisenman   Louis Danziger   George Tscherny

PRESIDENT   AWARD WINNER   CHAIRMAN

136

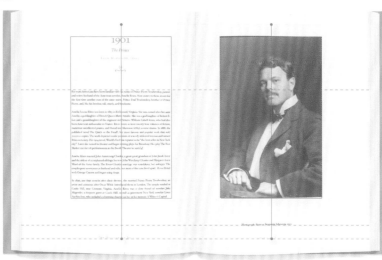

138

137

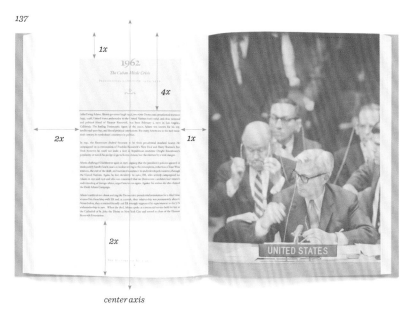

center axis

136, 137
History of Me book
with grid structure
and ratio notations
Sean Adams
2008

138, 139
History of Me book

139

Chapter 7: Pride

There are two sides to pride, and there are two motives for a designer to communicate pride. "Pride is the first sin, the source of all other sins, and the worst sin," according to Saint Thomas Aquinas, the thirteenth-century Doctor of the Church. In this definition, pride is an excessive desire for one's superiority over others, and according to Aquinas, God. Then there is the type of pride that is centered upon accomplishments and social achievements for the community. [140] Designers work with both sides of pride to communicate an idea and produce a reaction. Like elegance, pride relates to our culture and societal values. One may be proud to have twelve shrunken heads, while another would prefer a bowling trophy.

140

SAN FRANCISCO
2012

141

140
San Francisco
Olympics, 2012 poster
Jennifer Morla
2009

141
Berlin Olympics,
1936 poster
Ludwig Holwein
1936

142
They never thought
she'd land him!
Colgate advertisement
unknown
c. 1940

142

Professors of Psychology, Jessica Tracy, and Richard Robins define the two components of pride as "authentic" and "hubristic." Authentic pride relates to confidence and goals. Hubristic pride suggests arrogance and self-aggrandizing identity. This can be subverted with propaganda to promote the darker side of nationalism. {141} In a utopian world, we can imagine a society that values all individuals for who they are, regardless of wealth or status. However, in our culture, these things matter. Our self-image depends on our achievements.

Design helps us determine how to display our success and communicate it to others. Modern advertising often suggests that the consumer is not beautiful, successful, attractive, or popular but will become these things by using the product advertised. The audience is urged to purchase the product to avoid social embarrassment and to avoid being ostracized from the community—"If only I use the right toothpaste, others will stop avoiding me and like me." {142}

Good designers are exceptionally aware of the messages they create. And they are typically committed to the greater good rather than selling harmful products or promoting destructive ideas to appease our own or others' pride. In 2002, Milton Glaser wrote an essay, "12 Steps on the Graphic Designer's Road to Hell," examining a designer's responsibility and willingness to engage in unethical communication.

Glaser encouraged each designer to determine his or her level of discomfort by asking a series of twelve questions. These ranged from lesser evils, such as "Would you be willing to design a package to look more prominent on the shelf?" to the truly reprehensible, such as "Would you develop an ad for a product in which frequent use could result in the user's death?"

The essay spawned debate as some designers saw it as their job to be in service of any client, to remain neutral and objective. Others, including Glaser, argued that each of us has a set of values that should inform whom we choose to work with and what messages we create.

143
Thor's Fight with
the Giants painting
Mårten Eskil Winge
1872

144
Swing It Brother!
Don't Slow Up the
Ship poster
Paul Hesse
c. 1943

143

As a positive force for the community and others, designers can work with pride as a powerful motivational tool. Let us begin with national pride. During World War II, nations on both sides of the conflict increased military production. From 1939–45, the allied powers produced 55,000 ships and 640,000 airplanes. In comparison, in 1940, the year before the United States' entry into the war, the United States produced less than 3,000 military aircraft.

This level of production requires enormous resources. All consumer automobile and appliance manufacturing ceased. People built ships, planes, tanks, and military vehicles. The government enlisted as many men and women as possible. With a large population deployed in the military, manpower was in high demand.

A poster for ship production encourages faster production with three commands: "Swing it Brother!" a reference to swing dancing and music, "Don't give up the ship!" and "Keep 'em launching!" Commands are easy to understand. They do not ask us to make decisions nor create stress. They tell us what to do and when to do it.

144

145

146

147

148

145
Washington Dulles
International Airport
model
Eero Saarinen
1962

146
Los Angeles
International Airport
Theme Building
**William Pereira,
Charles Luckman,
Welton Becket, and
Paul R. Williams at
The Luckman
Partnership**
1961

147
Trans World Flight
Center, John F.
Kennedy Airport
model
Eero Saarinen
1956
photographer
Balthazar Korab

148
Trans World Airlines
logo
Raymond Loewy
1959

The photographer shot the ship-builder from below and shirtless to create a heroic stature. The hammer is a reference to the Norse god Thor for added power. [143] The ship-builder stands proudly in front of the shipyard construction and American flags, telling us that this is a patriotic and cooperative task. In contrast to much of the negative propaganda of the war that focused on denigrating the enemy, this poster promotes pride in work. [144]

Civic pride reflects a shared sense of identity and regional affiliation. It is demonstrated with the actions of local government, tribalism in sports, and public design. Before the advent of widespread air travel, railroad stations such as Gare du Nord in Paris, Antwerpen-Centraal in Antwerp, and Union Station in Washington DC demonstrated a city's pride. The railroad station was a traveler's first encounter with a town or city. A railroad station in a small town was often one of the community's best buildings and served as advertising for a city in order to promote economic growth.

In the twentieth century, airports introduced the traveler to a city. As air travel became widespread, cities and towns invested in their airports. Previously utilitarian administrative structures and a tower became architectural statements for each community. By the 1930s, more local visitors than passengers visited the airport. Berlin's airport included a restaurant seating 3,000 people on the roof of the terminal. The airport became a center of social activity.

The French anthropologist Marc Augé described the airport as a "non-place." A non-place has no identity or personality. Augé argues that airports, like fast-food chains, are the same everywhere. While this may be accurate for a significant number of airports, many are dramatic expressions of a region's identity.

In addition to serving as a transport hub, architects design airports to convey civic pride, stability, and grandeur. An airport, however, must also provide the traveler with a sense of security, safety, and calm.

Post-9/11, a traveler traverses a problematic course of check-in, security screening, document presentation, and finding a gate. Large volumes of space can reduce the sense of overcrowding. Wayfinding and schedule screens provide access to information and a stronger sense of self-control, reducing stress. Retail, dining, and exhibitions of local art minimize the aggravation of travel and supply local color.

The Los Angeles International Airport Theme Building stands as a symbol of the city's space-age optimistic thinking in 1961. [145] Washington Dulles international Airport's curvilinear roofline reflects the arc of a flight. [146] The vast expanses of glass recall great European Railroad stations. Architect Eero Saarinen designed Dulles with the automobile as a factor and created a sweeping roadway for the entrance. He added mobile lounges to transport the passengers to the plane, an innovative concept that matched the creative atmosphere of the early 1960s.

149
*Unemployed Lumber
Worker Goes with his
Wife to the Bean
Harvest* photograph
Dorothea Lange
1939

Eero Saarinen's design for the Trans World Flight Center at JFK Airport proudly echoed its corporate identity. {147, 148} The fluid forms also refer to a bird's wings and flight. As a gateway to the United States for international travelers, the terminal stood for optimism, new technologies, and TWA's willingness to be daring and innovative.

In 1935, at the height of the Great Depression, President Franklin D. Roosevelt signed the Social Security Act. The Act provided a "comprehensive package of protection" against the "hazards and vicissitudes of life": unemployment insurance, old-age assistance, aid to dependent children, and grants to the states to provide various forms of medical care. Part of the population disapproved of the Act as a socialist action. Others, often those in need, supported it with fervor.

Through the 1930s, Dorothea Lange traveled across the United States to document poverty, unemployment, the homeless, and the displaced for the federal government's Farm Security Administration. In Oregon, she photographed an unemployed lumber worker and his wife in their makeshift tent. Another photographer might only have shot the man with an ordinary headshot. Lange ingeniously created an asymmetrical composition with the man in focus while his wife is out of focus and darker in the background. Lange centers the viewer's gaze on the man's tattoo on his right arm. The tattoo is his social security number to show his support for the Social Security Act and pride of association with the program. {149} Of course, this was pre-identity theft; not such a good idea today.

Pride has positive evolutionary benefits. We feel pride when we achieve a goal. Consider life on the African savannah two hundred thousand years ago. If one's achievement had clear benefits for the social group, one would gain social advancement, additional resources, and better attract mates (the same is true today). This pattern continued as human beings developed larger communities. Civilization demands accomplishment and progress. Pride of achievement and reward from the community are necessary for this to succeed.

151

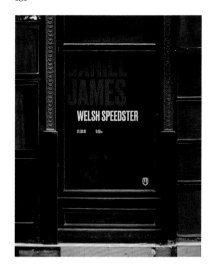

150
Manchester United
Footbal Club proposal
with a focus on
individuals and
broadcast schedule
Angad Singh
2019

151
Manchester United
Footbal Club proposal
street posters

However, pride and shame are bound together. Unless we are fortunate to reach a state of metaphysical rejection of the material world, we judge ourselves and others by accomplishment and material associations. Failure to meet a goal, or the threat of disappointing the group, leads to shame and embarrassment. The fear of losing social status is not merely a self-esteem issue. Imagine repeatedly failing at killing the lion. This could lead to rejection from the group and subsequent banish-ment and death. It is not surprising that one of the most common fears among all people is public speaking. The chance to fail before a large group may not be life-threatening, but we still carry the evolutionary fear of social rejection.

This primal emotion pairs with a strong connection to tribalism with sports fans. The feeling one has for the team of his or her choice is far more potent than a mere preference. The hard-core sports fan bonds emotionally with the team. It is his or her group that provides a sense of belonging. When a team wins, the fan shares in this with a team, basking in reflected glory. Fortunately, in sports, there will always be a winner and a loser in a game, unlike actual war or group conflict, where there may be no clear winner. When their team wins, he or she may say, "We won." If they lose, the statement changes to "They lost." Sports teams, then, must focus on winning to maintain the bond.

For a proposed cable network dedicated to the Manchester United Football Club, designer Angad Singh intensified the tribal language. {150, 151} "Glory earned," "We are Manchester United," and heroic statements such as, "All By Himself" pair with images of intense action by the team and the fans to create a combined sense of pride and belonging. The graphic language is sharp, intense, almost fascist, and seems to be screaming the words of victory. There is no middle ground in this successful system; one is a Manchester United fan, rightfully proud, or, one is the enemy.

Manchester United adopted recognisable language and symbols for clear messaging. Redefining symbols asks the viewer first to recognize the icon, and then reconsider his or her comprehension. The NBC peacock initially communicated color television. When NBC launched color television programming, NBC's Director of Design John Graham designed the logo. "The

152
NBC logo
Steff Geissbühler at
Chermayeff & Geismar
1986

153
Dear World:
Cambridge University
advertising campaign
Johnson Banks
2015

152

following program is brought to you in living color on NBC," accompanied the logo animation to associate the peacock with color. Historically, the peacock is not a symbol of color, but pride. When a male peacock courts, he spreads his feathers to attract a female, hence NBC's slogan, "Proud as a peacock."

Steff Geissbühler redesigned the logo used today, simplifying the forms. This version skillfully minimizes any complex shapes, echoing the same circle and angles throughout. The logo, merging color and pride now, is an extraordinary example of a symbol changing its meaning with dedicated and cohesive branding. {152}

To celebrate 800 years of achievement, Cambridge University commissioned Johnson Banks to develop a coherent theme for alumni and fundraising. Rather than following the expected course for a university that speaks to the future, ("Looking to the future," "Helping you reach your potential," and "Endless possibilities"), Johnson Banks looked at Cambridge's remarkable impact on the world. Allowing a college to boast with pride is a bold concept. Others will dissect

every statement of high achievement for veracity. Cambridge is one of the few universities in the world that can claim ownership of these statements with no sense of exaggeration. {153}

Now, here is how this can go wrong: the audience may perceive pride as elitist or arrogant. Johnson Banks averts this with the clever use of humor and understatement. The tone of the messages is informal, starting with "Dear World." The design aesthetic is unpretentious and friendly. The solution invites the viewer to solve the message and feel connected once he or she recognizes the idea, statement, or person mentioned.

Cambridge is a compelling example of the precarious line a designer walks communicating pride. If one is too strong, the message is boasting. If it is too quiet, the message is lost. When asked to define attributes for an organization, most CEOs will list excellence, quality, and success. Few companies want to convey failure. This ubiquitous hubris leads to screaming how fantastic the brand is to the world. Most consumers are more than cognizant that this is a marketing tactic and disregard the message.

153

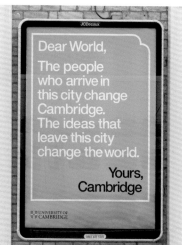

Dear World,

The people who arrive in this city change Cambridge. The ideas that leave this city change the world.

Yours, Cambridge

Dear Shakespeare, Stick at it, you have talent.

Yours, Marlowe

Christopher Marlowe (Corpus Christi College 1580), playwright and seminal influence on Shakespeare
cam.ac.uk/YoursCambridge

154

154
Planned Parenthood
environmental design
Paula Scher
2016

Planned Parenthood is an organization
dedicated to women's health issues,
including reproductive rights. The extraordinary activist for birth control Margaret
Sanger founded the organization in 1916
when she founded the first birth control
clinic in the United States—and was
immediately arrested. Since its founding,
the supporters of Planned Parenthood
demonstrated, marched, and campaigned
for women's health issues.

Paula Scher embraced the century-long
struggle and its victories for the environmental graphics for the headquarters. With
bold colors and exaggerated scale, Scher
recontextualized elements of the organization's printed matter and photography into
a vibrant and unapologetic stance of pride
and determination. {154}

For an annual report for the Academy of
Motion Picture Arts and Sciences, I did not
boast of the extraordinary work of the
Academy. I listed factual figures printed
with Academy gold and designed for variety
and visual impact. The viewer can decide if
these numbers are impressive or not (they
are). Once the viewer makes a determination based on evidence, he or she is more
likely to accept the success as credible. {156}

156

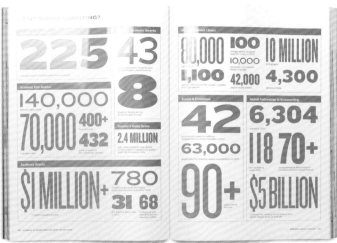

155

155
*Washington Crossing
the Delaware*
Emanuel Leutze
1851

156
2011 Annual Report
for the Academy of
Motion Picture Arts
and Sciences
Sean Adams
2011

157
*Washington Crossing
the Delaware* (detail)

157

Conversely, the artist Emanuel Leutze's artistic liberties for his painting, *Washington Crossing the Delaware*, emphasize the role of hyperbole. {155} To accentuate the heroic and mythic, Leutze stands Washington taller than any other passenger. His face is sharp and clear on the one bright background of the painting. The other people on the boat represent the American population at the time, to convey the unity of the nation: a Scottish man, two farmers, an African American, a Native American, and a woman dressed in men's clothing. {157}

The large gold frame depicts the American eagle and crest, stars, and a line from Washington's eulogy by Henry Lee, "First in war, first in peace and first in the hearts of his countrymen." The combination of the subject, composition, and frame illustrates the goal of the artist to convey pride. This amount of theatrical representation and drama works with national pride, but rarely for a new car campaign or appliance advertising.

Chapter 8: Innovation

Humans are naturally innovative. Neanderthals created tools but made no changes or advances for over one hundred thousand years. About eighty thousand years ago, *Homo sapiens*, alternatively, began building new tools and art forms. Tied with our ability to communicate with language and pass knowledge on to the next generation, this gave us a huge advantage. We intuitively look at a process or tool and determine if a different approach might work better. Translating the essential human trait of innovating new ideas that can be transmitted, designed, built, produced, and understood, is the hard part.

158

159

158
Pivotal environmental
design
Ian Lynam Design
2016

159
Pivotal icon detail

160
Expo Buenos
Aires 2023
campaign
Hueso
2019

Few organizations want to be considered unimaginative and bored with future possibilities. A client rarely says, "No, I don't want to do anything new." Unfortunately, most companies insist that they are innovative and future-oriented, but they are not—real innovation pairs with risk. One must be willing to try something previously never considered or previously thought to be nuts. Of course, there are many organizations where innovation is a driving principle, and they try new ideas, processes, products, and technology. It takes courage to choose the path less taken.

Creativity drives innovation. This is frightening to people who work with absolutes. Change is an idea that cannot be artificial. The audience is aware that just slapping "New" on a package does not make something new. There are a plethora of design solutions that appear avant-garde, cutting edge, and alternative. To believe that something is genuinely Promethean, we need proof in action.

Forms that signify innovation change depending on the era. In the 1980s, new-wave design suggested fresh thinking and ideas. The designers who led the path created genuinely original work that

challenged modernism and looked for new technologies as tools. But, like all movements, the approach became a style adopted by everything targeted to a young audience. Once the forms hit the school Trapper Keeper, it is probably over.

In the 1990s, grunge design followed the same trajectory. In the 2000s, designers celebrated minimalism for anything fresh and new. Currently, big typographic words broken apart randomly, flat geometric shapes, and biomorphic design suggest inventive modern ideas. However, the only work that is truly innovative is based on an understanding of history, culture, social issues, and ideas previously considered unacceptable.

Communicating a sophisticated and innovative product requires translation. For example, Pivotal is an organization that "accelerates the digital transformation of the world's largest companies with a modern software development methodology and modern cloud platform." Innovation and creativity are inherent in the product. Ian Lynam designed the interior graphics for Pivotal's Tokyo offices. He translated their multiple services and platforms into

visuals. Lynam created a library of "anti-patterns." These icons combine lesser-known Japanese characters, discarded characters from Japanese orthographic reform in 1946, and symbols from the Japanese landscape. [158, 159]

Lynam layered the characters and symbols together, along with characters from other dead languages. This created a new iconographic language that visualizes the generative and entropic characteristics of any language. The hundreds of anti-patterns line the walls of the offices, encouraging the viewer to decipher them and find an organizational structure; in fact, try to learn the language. The viewer's process is a microcosm of Pivotal's work.

For a proposed visual system for Expo Buenos Aires 2023, the Brazilian firm Hueso combined flat graphic shapes and three-dimensional elements to convey progress, the future, and new technology with a Brazilian vernacular. The symbols, from a mid-century atom to the sun, work with the viewer's recognition of the forms relating to innovation. Hueso brilliantly incorporates a bright and joyful palette pointing to a utopian, rather than dystopian future. [160]

160

161

$48 Billion worth of food
was thrown out last year.
A smarter planet needs
smarter food systems.
Let's build a smarter planet.
ibm.com/think

THINK

Retailers lose 93 billion every year
because they don't have the
right inventory in stock.
A smarter planet needs
smarter retail systems.
Let's build a smarter planet.
ibm.com/think

THINK

Every year people burn 2.3 billion
gallons of fuel sitting in traffic.
A smarter planet needs
smarter traffic systems.
Let's build a smarter planet.
ibm.com/think

THINK

As the world becomes more interconnected,
fast-paced and unpredictable, cities are
struggling to protect their citizens.
A smarter planet needs smarter public safety.
Let's build a smarter planet.
ibm.com/think

THINK

1.5 million people in the U.S. are harmed every year due to medical prescriptions errors. A smarter planet needs smarter healthcare systems. Let's build a smarter planet. **ibm.com**/think

THINK

We can only extract about one-third of the oil in our existing reservoirs. A smarter planet needs smarter oil and gas fields. Let's build a smarter planet. **ibm.com**/think

THINK

161
Think IBM campaign
**Office: Jason Schulte
Design**
2008

Iconography served a different, but no less creative solution for IBM. In the mid-2000s, IBM recognized the opportunity to provide leadership solving some of the world's most significant issues. That's a tall order. The team at Office visualized the massive undertaking in forms that are approachable, friendly, and globally recognizable. Starting with the spirit of Paul Rand's designs for IBM, Office designed icons in flat shapes. But, fifty years after Rand's work, the world is a different place. Office's solution reflects the past, but reinterprets iconography for a modern audience. {161}

As opposed to the typical consumer in 1960, we have interfaced with iconography for most of our lives. Those born post-iPhone have never known a world without flat and bright icons. Subsequently, the audience today can recognize and decode much more complex iconography quickly and efficiently. Office's visual language works in print and on screen. It is static, in motion, or interactive. The bright and optimistic tone conceals the depth of research, innovation in form, and conceptual advances in the system. It does exactly what it is meant to: present a friendly face that communicates possibilities while addressing deeply labyrinthian issues.

162
Trylon and Perisphere:
New York World's Fair
Wallace Harrison, and
J. André Fouilhoux
1939
Photographer:
Samuel H. Gottscho

162

In the built environment, if a structure is oddly shaped, we see innovation. Some buildings are incredibly innovative with construction, technology, and sustainability, but don't "look" innovative.

Nevertheless, when a building is a sphere or a giant triangle, it signals to the onlooker that it is magnificently advanced. The 1939 New York World's Fair Trylon and Perisphere stood as icons at the center of the fair. The pavilion housed a diorama designed by Henry Dreyfuss depicting "The World of Tomorrow," a model of the city of the future. For the visitor, the structures represented a utopian tomorrow signified by their pure geometry and gleaming white surface. In reality, traditional construction issues created a range of problems, resulting in compromises to the design. {162}

The Trylon and Perisphere created our expectation for geometric diversity and innovation. In 1960, Brazil moved the capital from Rio de Janeiro to a site more centrally located in the Amazon. Lúcio Costa, Oscar Niemeyer, and Joaquim Cardozo planned, developed, and designed the city to represent Brazil's utopian future. Oscar Niemeyer designed the buildings with bold horizontal lines and contrasting circular or curved shapes. Many of the structures appear to float off the surface, suspended above the earth. Like the Trylon and Perisphere, the smooth white surfaces project unity and purity. {163}

Seven years later, Moshe Safdie designed Habitat 67 for the Montreal Expo '67. The stacked cube structure appears futuristic and almost alien. Safdie's intent, however, was not only to communicate innovation to the public but to reinvent the idea of apartment living. The Metabolism movement's founders believed that architects should design a city or building like an organic system with individual cells and interconnections. Safdie, influenced by Metabolism and Le Corbusier's use of materials, designed the apartment building to, as he explained, "Give the qualities of a house to each unit—habitat would be all about gardens, contact with nature, streets instead of corridors." {164}

163

164

165
Sayl Chair
Yves Béhar
2010

166
Bayer Intelligent
interactive packaging
proposal
Angela Baek
2019

165

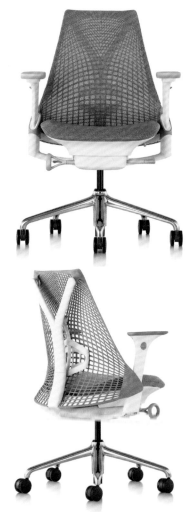

Yves Béhar's Sayl Chair for Herman Miller shows that we can transfer the concept of unexpected geometric forms to convey innovation in other design practices. Béhar, who lives in San Francisco, designed the chair based on the structure of the Golden Gate Bridge, a suspension bridge. He applied the same engineering principles and reinvented the possibilities of an office chair. The unframed suspension back and elastic material allow the user to have a wide range of motion with less mechanical parts. The chair uses fewer materials to produce and maintain Herman Miller's commitment to eco-friendly practices. The economy of material also keeps the costs of the chair lower, matching the price of an office chair at an office supply store. The geometry and construction appear innovative, like Habitat 67—they are. [165]

Allied to real innovators like Safdie and Béhar, Angela Baek tackled the issues of over-the-counter medication. She determined that ongoing problems included confusion between brands and products, dosage information, and product expiration. Fortunately, Baek looked beyond a cleaner typographic system to solve the issues. She proposed a combination of interactive intelligence and packaging to make self-diagnosis and self-treatment easier for those seeking pain relief. [166]

The in-store kiosk and mobile phone will serve as a "one minute clinic" for the user to find the products suitable for their body type and symptoms. The product's labels act as touch screens for easier access to information, typically remarkably tiny on the back. And finally, the products and mobile system sync with smart home devices. The radical innovation in the process of purchasing over-the-counter medication is hidden. Baek's visual solution beautifully minimizes fear and stress with bright colors, friendly icons, and highly legible typography.

In 2014, trend forecaster Lidewij Edelkoort curated an exhibition for the Design Museum Holon, Israel exploring craft and contemporary design. Long considered a lesser medium, craft is a modern movement that questions mass production and the homogenization of global culture. In the exhibition, Edelkoort combined current design themes with authentic handmade crafts stating, "It is time for mending and gathering, thus restoring the fabric of

166

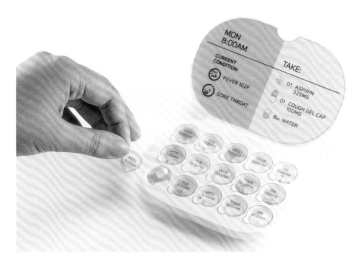

167

168

167
Poster for *Gathering*
exhibition at Design
Museum Holon
Kobi Franco
2014

168
Into The Black Mirror
publication
Kizzy Memani
2017

society: picking up the pieces and bringing them together in a patchwork of possibilities; a quilt of substance, able to absorb shock and fear." Kobi Franco's posters for the exhibition articulate the intervention of new technologies and in domestic craft. The forms speak to creation and possibilities with the bright central merged image, white background, and crisp typography in English and Hebrew. {167}

This redefining of media or concept is a constant in all innovation. The designer is faced with the challenge of communicating the message in graphic, screen-based designs, products, or environments, that the new concept is valid and accessible. Franco's poster utilizes multiple images and typography in two languages to manage this message.

A publication by South African designer Kizzy Memani speaks to the subject, Afrofuturism, with straightforward typography. Afrofuturism is a concept that navigates the complexities of African diaspora with culture, aesthetics, technology, and science fiction. Memani's cover tells the story elegantly. Reflective silver typography on a deep matte black background allows us to see "something on

nothing" and also see ourselves. The typographic forms reflect traditional African patterns through a future-oriented lens of high technology. Rather than providing the answer, Memani's cover invites the viewer to explore the content on the inside. {168}

Oddly, one of the best examples of design, innovation, culture, and technology is the occasional or coffee table. It is a standard piece of furniture with little to do but be a surface for books, magazines, cups, and feet. Let's walk through this, starting with a table from Rome built around 1720. The decoration of this table displays the elaborate style of the Baroque in Rome. Only the rich could afford the hand-carved forms and gilding. This is an object to display wealth and social status. {169} In 1929, Mies van der Rohe designed the Barcelona table following modernist tenets of the Bauhaus. The metal and glass construction hides nothing. Van der Rohe hoped to innovate furniture that brought good design to the masses with egalitarian forms. Unfortunately, the production proved to be complicated. The Barcelona

table was and is not inexpensive. {170} Isamu Noguchi's table appealed to the public with biomorphic shapes in response to the hard forms and metal of World War II. Production innovations kept costs lower. Herman Miller produced the table from 1947–73, then restarted in 1980. It is still in production today. {171} Similarly, the Eames Elliptical table, referred to as the "surfboard," followed the biomorphic form with a new manufacturing technique for welding wire-rod bases together. The Eameses created the base for the table to host a traditional Japanese tea ceremony at their house in California. This requires sitting on the floor. The Elliptical table extended this invitation with its low profile matching the need for more casual entertaining in post-war America and Europe without live-in household help. {172}

In 1957, Eero Saarinen determined to "clear up the slum of legs" he saw in the home. Based on the shape of a drop of liquid, he designed the Saarinen Tulip Table. The curved forms managed to appeal to consumers through the 1950s with its organic forms, the 1960s space-age flavor, 1970s plastic forms, through to today. {173}

1720

169
Italian side table
unknown
1720–1730

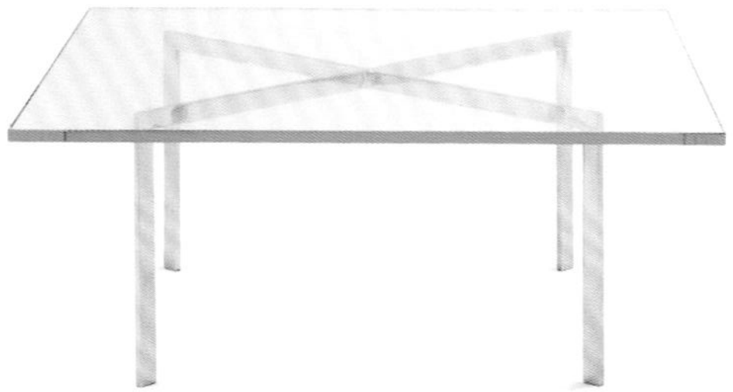

1929

170
Bacelona Table
Ludwig Mies van der Rohe
1929

1947

171
Noguchi Table
Isamu Noguchi
1947

1951

172
Eames Wire Base
Elliptical Table
Charles and Ray Eames
1951

1957

173
Saarinen Coffee Table
Eero Saarinen
1957

1960

174
Eames Walnut Stools
Charles and Ray Eames
1960

1978

175
I-Beam Table
Ward Bennett
1978

2018

176
Plinth Table
Norm Architects
2018

177

177, 178
There Are No Homosexuals in Iran book
Thuy-An Hoang, Xavier Erni, and Laurence Rasti at Neo Neo
2017

Ray Eames designed the Eames walnut stool in 1959 for the Time-Life Building in New York. Trained as a painter and sculptor, she developed three stool forms that work together as a place to sit, a table, or as she used them in the Eames House, a spot for plants and collections.[174]

The 1970s introduced the high-tech industrial style to residential design. The style celebrated innovation and honesty with exposed pipes, restaurant equipment, and functional commercial furniture. Ward Bennett's I-Beam table is a masterpiece of architectural and industrial precision, crafted from powder-coated cast aluminum.[175] Lastly, Norm Architects' Plinth Table reflects the consumer's desire for minimalist shapes.[176] As a straightforward slab or cube of marble, the table combines austere restraint with the softness of the marble.

The tables illustrate the ways that culture affects design. New forms followed as urban living changed to suburban life, and people evolved their social habits. New technologies, developed from conflict, allowed for new processes and solutions. Innovation is not always a polite and gentle path of step-by-step invention.

Then there is social innovation. In this sphere, the designer works with established visual forms that create a bridge between two ideas. Social change occurs when individual human relationships and communication slowly change larger cultural and social constructs. A top-down demand for change fails. It is only when we meet and communicate with someone from the "other" group that we modify our thinking. The call for LGBTQ+ individuals to "come out" recognizes that once someone realizes that the person they know is gay, bisexual, or trans, he or she will change their negative preconceptions.

Neo Neo tackled the issue of homosexuality in Iran with a book of Laurence Rasti's photographs. Rasti's work explores the hybridization of her Iranian heritage and Swiss upbringing. The images in *There Are No Homosexuals in Iran* are a response to a statement by former Iranian President Mahmoud Ahmadinejad, "In Iran, we do not have homosexuals like in your country."

Rasti photographed gay refugees from Iran in a small town in Turkey. Neo Neo partners, Thuy-An Hoang and Xavier Erni, designed the cover to state the content plainly, surrounded by Islamic patterns. On the inside, they present the images to promote a personal connection. By allowing the images to bleed off the pages with no text, the designers invite the viewer into the content. The minimal solution allows him or her to consider it with no interruption. The result is a personal experience with the book as an object in one's hand—the beginnings of social change.[177, 178]

In 2017, the Cervantes Institute in Madrid published *Fresh Latino 2* about young Spanish and Latin American architects. The curator, Ariadna Cantis and architect Andrés Jaque provided ten terms to characterize the architects, including: disengage, dispute, empowerment, re-appropriation, and resilience.

Florencia Grassi and Leandro Lattes designed the exhibition and publication reflecting on the terms. The visual language appears to be in a state of flux.[179] There is no fixed typographic element—the identity changes with no apparent logic. Grassi and Lattes beautifully articulate innovation with the sensation of being unbalanced and open to alternative forms and ideas.

178

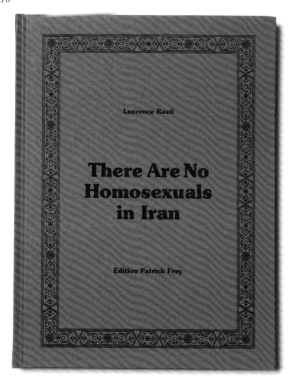

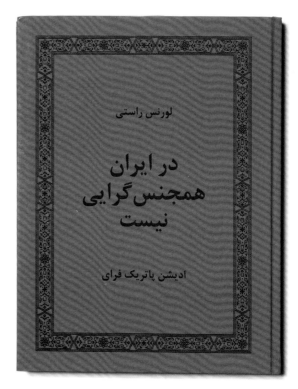

179
Identity for *Fresh
Latino 2* exhibition
**Florencia Grassi and
Leandro Lattes at
El Vivero**
2013–15

freeeeeeshhhhlatino^{oooooo} 2   fressshhhhhlalala
la la tino 2   fffrrreeeeeshlalalatino.2   frrrr
frfr fre e esh ¡latino! 2   fresh sh sh sh latin
latinolatino 2   frrrrreshshshshshlatino!2   fre
fresh la tino 2   fresh latino 2   fffff fresh l
freshla^{la}la^{la}tino 2   fre e e e e sh la ti no 2

     fffffresh la la la tino 2   fffffresh la
shshlatino!2   fresh fresh latino......2
fresh la latino ooooooo 2   freshfresh
 latino o$^{o^{o}o^{o}o}$ 2   fresh la ti no 2
2222222   freshlatino 2
 e e sh lala ti no 2

Chapter 9: Innocence

Innocence is not ignorance. Innocence is a positive state that comes from a lack of sophistication, wickedness, knowledge, and guile. Lambs and children are innocent. Not learning algebra is not innocent. When we consider the idea of innocence, we assume simplicity, lack of intellectual depth, and safety. This comes with visual preconceptions: bright primary colors, basic shapes such as triangles, squares, and circles, and in a worst-case scenario, fake chalkboard typefaces with a backward *S*. These visual tropes imply that the viewer is stupid, a toddler, or both. Innocence can be communicated with much more sophistication.

180

YEAR-ROUND YOUNG BEAUTY

180
Seventeen magazine
Cipe Pineles
1948
Photographer:
Ben Somoroff

181
Wide Awake Library
periodical
Frank Tousey
1895

182
A Family Group
unknown
c. 1850

182

181

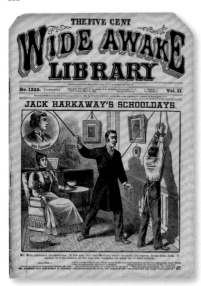

Interestingly, while we associate childhood with innocence, Victorian society believed the opposite. [182] Children were born inherently evil and required constant discipline to become civilized people, hence the term, "I'll beat the devil out of you." [181] By the mid-1950s, parents had revised the concept, considering babies blank slates ready to be taught how to behave. The relationship between innocence and sexuality is a long-standing and typically sexist idea and subtext in much design conveying innocence. Western culture and religion promoted the idea that a girl is innocent until her first sexual experience and a woman who commits adultery is no longer innocent. In contrast, men who lose their virginity are respected and considered to have fulfilled their masculine agenda.

The idea of the teenager is a mid-twentieth century invention. By the 1940s, people between thirteen and eighteen were no longer small adults ready for the field or factory. This was a new market for products and entertainment. *Seventeen* magazine debuted in 1944. The first editor, Helen Valentine, managed the content to equip teenage girls with the information

and tools necessary to have a career. The magazine also included articles on health, relationships, and other parts of a young girl's life.

In 1947, Valentine hired Cipe Pineles as one of the first woman art directors of a major magazine. Pineles helped craft the publication to be at the forefront of design, photography, and illustration. She recognized that young women were not silly and clueless, but smart, ambitious, and serious. The July 1948 cover connotes the natural elements of a young woman's life in the summer. The branches, leaves, and shells dance around the model's face as if they were a Calder mobile. Pineles was exceptionally skilled at composition with multiple objects. The combination of the images on the cover elegantly reveals a glimpse of a young woman's innocence and invoking a carefree summer. [180]

Alexander Girard captured the same light, playful, and fresh tone with the color wheel ottoman. Girard designed the ottoman to be a coffee table, footrest, or extra seat. Its flexible usage adds to the casual tone in opposition to a heavy leather ottoman that says, "I'm an ottoman. Only." The top

183

183
Girard Color Wheel
Ottoman
Alexander Girard
1967

184
Pepsi-Cola World
publication
**Brownjohn,
Chermayeff &
Geismar**
1960

185
Island of Soil
packaging
**Yuma Harada and
Yuka Tsuda at UMA /
design farm**
2016

suggests a pinwheel in motion. The low
profile is unpretentious and inviting. The
thin legs provide a sense of lightness as if it
were floating in the room. {183}

As Pineles did on her *Seventeen* cover,
Brownjohn, Chermayeff, and Geismar
conveyed the season, spring, with elements
that might belong in a child's treasure box.
{184} The idea of communicating an identity
with only inanimate objects is an ingenious
concept. The viewer is allowed to imagine
him or herself as the owner of the treasures
and create a personal narrative. The items,
like the objects in the Lustig *3 Tragedies*
cover, force us to imagine the connections.
Each piece provides a clue to understanding our version of the story. But, whatever
narrative we imagine in this case, one thing
is clear: that kid drinks a lot of Pepsi.

Organic fertilizer is not a standard product
that one connects to innocence. But UMA /
design farm in Osaka, Japan, designed
packaging for Island of Soil with wit and
play. The studio worked with traditional
elements of agricultural packaging:
straightforward and unadorned typography, minimal imagery, and one color
printing. They augmented these and
changed the tone from banal to novel and

184

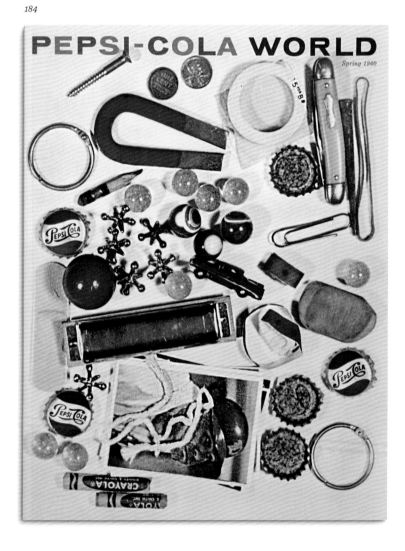

185

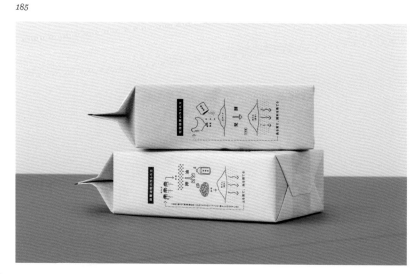

186

KANTO TOUR GUIDE
Tour 9 of 10!
Tokyo | 1 day
港区 by カーレン・クンツ
MINATO CITY by KAAREN KUNZE

KANTO TOUR GUIDE
Tour 8 of 10!
Tokyo | 1 day
有楽町 by ジャン・スノー
YURAKUCHO by JEAN SNOW

KANTO TOUR GUIDE
Tour 4 of 10!
Tokyo | 1 day
渋谷 by ヴィヴィアン・モレリ
SHIBUYA by VIVIAN MORELLI

KANTO TOUR GUIDE
Tour 5 of 10!
Tokyo | 2 day
新島 by スザンナ・ベア
NIIJIMA by SUSANNA BAER

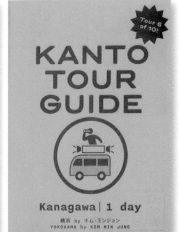

KANTO TOUR GUIDE
Tour 6 of 10!
Kanagawa | 1 day
横浜 by キム・ミンジョン
YOKOHAMA by KIM MIN JUNG

KANTO TOUR GUIDE
Tour 3 of 10!
Tokyo | 1 day
世田谷 by アレックス・ゾンダレッガー
SETAGAYA by ALEX SONDEREGGER

KANTO TOUR GUIDE
Tour 2 of 10!
Tokyo | 1 day
杉並 by ジャレド・ブレイタマン
SUGINAMI by JARED BRAITERMAN

KANTO TOUR GUIDE
Tour 1 of 10!
Tokyo | 1 day
東海道（日本橋〜品川）by ルーカス・B.B.
Tokaido by Lucas Badtke-Berkow

KANTO TOUR GUIDE
Tour 7 of 10!
Tokyo | 1 day
沢井 by クリス・バーテルセン
SAWAI by CHRIS BERTHELSEN

187

186–187
*Kanto Tour Guide:
Tokyo*
**Ian Lynam and
Thien Huynh**
2016

dynamic. The pastel colors and lighthearted icons communicate the tone. UMA adds one more step: the elements create a face on the front of the packaging. The design is mischievous and unexpected for this industry but makes perfect sense. {185}

Shibaura House in Tokyo is a shared workspace for the local community and international visitors. The building is the center of multiple cultural programs, hosting everything from cooking to English classes and visiting lecturers. To connect local residents and global guests to Tokyo, Shibaura House published a series of guides, each curated by a different prominent member of the Tokyo community. Ian Lynam and Thien Huynh designed the guides, producing them with the Risograph process, a low-cost photocopying printing technology.

Many travel guide books are printed with glossy paper and include professional photography of local landmarks. Icons and different colors of text make the dense information clear. When well designed, these guides are masterpieces of information design. But these are for the serious tourist, intent on seeing all the highlights with limited time.

188
Nut Tree icons
possibly Don Burrell
1971

189
Happy Pills candy
packaging
**Marion Dönneweg,
Merche Alcalá,
Jorge Virgós, and
Mireia Roda at
Estudio m**
2018

190
Fisher Price Portable
Gramophone
Fisher Price
1983
photographer
Tracy Sorel

191
Nelson Ceramic Clock
George Nelson
1953

192
Primary colors: yellow,
red, blue; and
secondary colors:
orange, green, purple

188

189

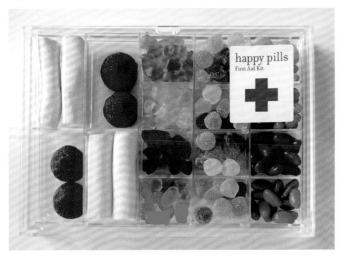

190

192

191

193

194

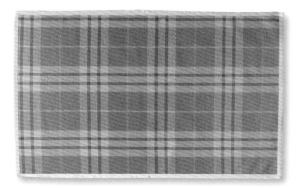

193
New England motif
dish towel
Pat Prichard
c. 1955

194
Taupe and grey dish
towel
Katarina Wiedtman
2002

Conversely, The Kanto Tour Guide's color palette of bright and upbeat colors minimizes the anxiety of navigating an enormous city like Tokyo. The lo-fi printing process and simple iconography signify a casual and spontaneous experience. The information appears timely and up-to-the-minute, like a newspaper. A coffee shop listed here may not be open in a month. Lynam and Huynh's iconography is critical. The starburst sun recalls a "New!" sticker. The circle surrounding the symbols references children's books or diagrams in textbooks. Every element is accessible and undemanding, presenting a childlike curiosity and genuine excitement. {100, 101}

Bright primary and secondary colors are common in design about excitement, fun, innocence, and children. They add a light, playful quality. {188–191} Based on Donald Norman's theory of visceral responses (Chapter 1, "Seduction"), these colors are easier for the brain to process. Since people prefer easy choices, primary colors ask less of us. {192} One knows that the stop sign is red. If it were pink, we would need to consider whether it was an orange or blue pink, closer to red or magenta. Primary and secondary colors only ask us to identify them: red, yellow, blue, and so on.

Then there is the type of innocence that relates to nostalgia. An old object or idea appears innocent to us compared to one from our own time. We comment on these items, "Isn't it funny someone thought this was sophisticated?" or "People sure were easily entertained." Innocence, in this regard, has the same qualities that we assign to children who are innocent because they don't have the knowledge of the "real" world. The innocent artifacts come from a time before ours when life, in memory, was more straightforward and less complicated. Humans are good at remembering the best and forgetting the bad in the past.

The Pat Prichard dish towel appears naïve. {193} Granted, dish towels are typically rather harmless and can be used without guilt, but this one lacks sophistication in contrast to a serious dish towel. {194} First, the pink background relates to childhood. The iconography to represent the subject, New England, is obvious and harmless (except for the lobsters): clam chowder, a lobster pot, sailing ships, clams, and baked beans. Prichard drew houses from the eighteenth century when life was seemingly simpler to the audience in the 1950s. She

illustrated the icons in a cartoon-like, humorous style with odd angles, clumsy letterforms, and no perspective. The overall effect is cheerful and playful. These elements and the connection to a seemingly less problematic time convey innocence and an escape from modern problems.

The illustrator and designer Arjen Klinkenberg (Polderkind) executed the logo for Club Geluk with the same "gee-whiz" and innocent style as the Prichard towel. Club Geluk is an Amsterdam-based organization dedicated to handcrafts such as macramé and embroidery, with a specialization in knitting.

Klinkenberg's logo projects an offbeat attitude with cues that this is safe and friendly: the awkward handwritten and playful letterforms, four-leaf clover on the inside of the *C*, and a swash *G* that creates a smile. {197}

The knit and crochet work, however, is not your grandmother's afghan blanket or scarf. Club Geluk publishes books on yarn and knitting, including *Yarn Porn*, patterns for "Your home-made hotness: a condom, genitals, pasties, tampons and more." The book *Club Geluk and The Secret of The*

195
Club Geluk:
Gebreide Kaasplank,
Gebreid vlees en vis,
Gebreide garnalen
pasta, Gebreide oesters
yarn sculptures
Marieke Voorsluijs
and Barbara Löhnen
2017
photographer
Brigitte Kroone

196
Club Geluk: *Ontbijt*
met ham yarn
sculpture

197
Club Geluk logo
Arjen Klinkenberg
2016

Knitted Ham and More Bizarre Knits
includes knitting patterns of lipsticks,
sneakers, peanut butter, crockery, ham,
and other nonsense. {195}.

Here, knitting and crochet remake
ordinary and everyday objects into
innocent and playful forms. Knitted
textiles have inherent associations with
the handmade and personal. These are
often items made with love for a relative.
Club Geluk's work asks the viewer to
reimagine a plate of pasta and shrimp, a
cuckoo clock, or ham as humorous and
slightly nonsensical. Slamming two
disconnected ideas together with sweet
and soft material beautifully reframes both
crochet and knitting and a ham or other
breakfast items. {196}

The International Conservation Caucus
Foundation (ICCF) lobbies for animal and
environmental conservation. To promote
ICCF to United States Senators and
Congress, the strategist Samantha
Fleming and I suggested a poster for
elementary schools. The poster solves two
issues: first, it helps children become aware
of the problems of issues around conservation and second, it encourages constituents
with children to contact their lawmakers.

195

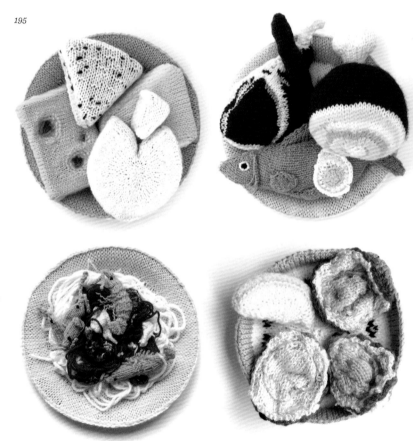

197

196

198

199

I designed a poster to educate children on the terms used for groups of animals. A long list is dull, but illustrating each word typographically maintained the tone of fun and play. {198} Nobody enjoys being lectured and told he or she is bad.

The Revival Remedy packaging has a similar tone for a different purpose. This is a package for hangover help. Today it seems odd to promote alcoholism, but it was considered funny when Harold's Club, a casino in Reno, produced this product in 1967. The design style is fluid and fanciful, with a touch of the Wild West. In 1967, it was no doubt seen as an innocent, but helpful, joke. The multiple Victorian typefaces and swirls read as comical. A black container with minimal sans serif typography might appear rather dangerous and suggest a more profound problem if the hangover cure is needed daily. {199}

Designing for children tends to bring out the inane in designers. The first stop on the train is the type with a backward *S*. This presumes that children are really, really stupid. They're not. When I was asked to rebrand Nickelodeon, my first goal was to treat children with respect. Like teenagers and adults, they enjoy a good story, can

recognize a good idea, and enjoy being challenged, not pandered to. Children are innocent, but that does not suggest they are sweet, sugary, and angelic. I followed this dictate with Nickelodeon, maintaining the brand's commitment to irreverence.

The graphic system stripped away any excess decoration, meaningless illustration, and a color palette that was so broad as to never be proprietary. The new approach, kid modernism, demanded bold and direct solutions. With no extraneous elements, any creative working with the system would need an idea, not just a chaotic layout. The typography was deliberately legible as part of the audience might be learning to read. {200} The aggressive design allowed for an irreverent tone, such as logo shapes simulating spit. On-screen graphics included things kids like, such as passing-gas sounds.

The one omission in the system, to maintain a measure of innocence and respect for the audience, was violence. There was no humor based on a cartoon character repeatedly hit with an oversized hammer or smashed with a boulder.

200

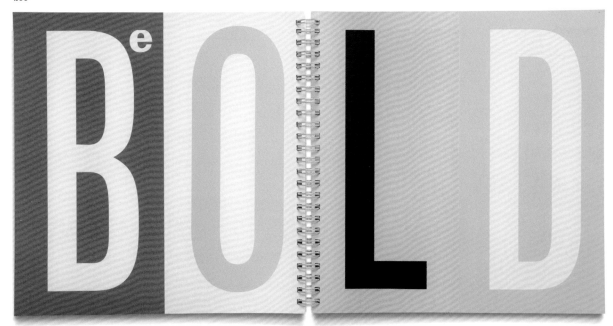

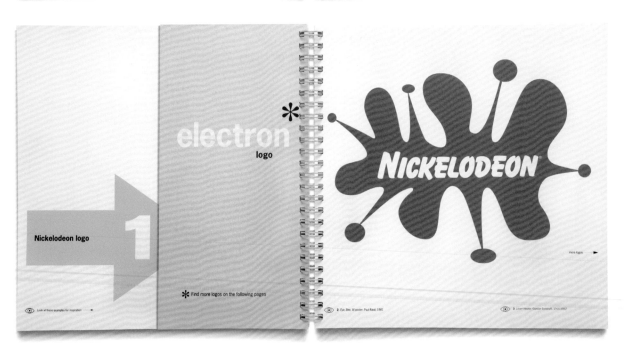

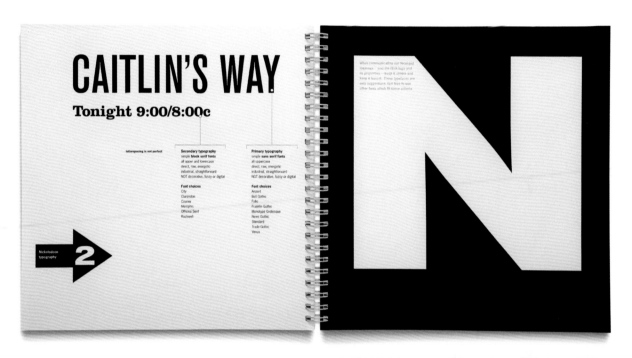

CAITLIN'S WAY

Tonight 9:00/8:00c

letterspacing is not perfect

Secondary typography
simple **block serif fonts**
all upper and lowercase
direct, raw, energetic
industrial, straightforward
NOT decorative, fussy or digital

Font choices
City
Clarendon
Courier
Memphis
Officina Serif
Rockwell

Primary typography
simple **sans serif fonts**
all uppercase
direct, raw, energetic
industrial, straightforward
NOT decorative, fussy or digital

Font choices
Airport
Bell Gothic
Folio
Franklin Gothic
Monotype Grotesque
News Gothic
Standard
Trade Gothic
Venus

Nickelodeon
typography

2

When communicating our focused
message - and the block logo and
its properties - keep it simple and
keep it honest. These typefaces are
only suggestions; feel free to use
other fonts which fit these criteria.

N

KID MODERNISM

Aggressive

Bold   Honest

Vibrant.   Clean

Direct   Bigger Than Life

Irreverent

201

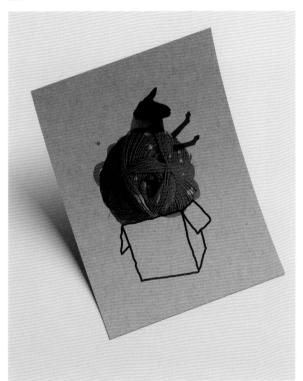

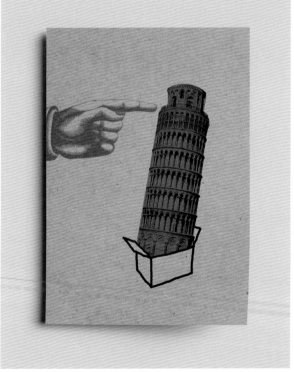

201
Little Big Kids flyers
Marion Dönneweg
2017

202
The Blind Are Also
Color Blind poster
**Carson/Roberts
Advertising**
c. **1958**
Photographer:
Doug Wilson

202

THE BLIND ARE ALSO COLOR BLIND

CARSON / ROBERTS / INC / *Advertising* / *Los Angeles*

Marion Dönneweg's work for Little Big Kids respects a child's intelligence and curiosity. For the bilingual center for children and creativity in Barcelona, Dönneweg minimized verbiage and created a series of visual puzzles, puns, and witticisms. Cardboard boxes inspired the craft paper material and simple two-color printing. The box, as a metaphor, guides much of the concept. As Dönneweg explains, "The box is a beautiful metaphor to explain all these little worlds, and seeing a box one can't help wondering what will be inside and want to open it to reveal the mystery." The project maintains the innocence and excitement of childhood with intellect. {201}

Again, innocence does not equate with complete ignorance. A 1958 poster by the Carson/Roberts Advertising to combat racism deftly portrays childlike innocence as a virtue to be follow. {202}

Chapter 10: Nostalgia

Guy de Maupassant said, "Our memory is a more perfect world than the universe: it gives back life to those who no longer exist." J. M. Barrie said, "God gave us memory so that we might have roses in December." Both of these statements define nostalgia. Our memories are rather weak. Every time we remember an event, we rewrite the memory. Furthermore, our emotions help us forget the negative and recall the positive. Nostalgia is what we feel when an object, sound, smell, or words prompt a longing for an idealized past we manufacture. The artifact itself plays a minor role in the process. It is only a trigger that prompts our memory of an interaction or relationship recalled fondly.

203

The Iron Horse
by
Paul Detlefsen

203
The Iron Horse printed
lithograph
Paul Detlefsen
1954

204
Photograph of the
author's great
grandfather
**Phillips and
Bergstresser**
1890

205
Filmforum newsletter
photograph of
Lupe Vélez from
Cine-Mundial
Sean Adams
1994

The book, *The Meaning of Things,* by
Mihály Csikszentmihalyi and Eugene
Rochberg-Halton, is a sublime exploration
of artifacts and nostalgia. The authors
visited different homes and asked the
inhabitants to identify their "special"
objects. The residents chose items, not for
monetary value, but based on their personal
connections and memories. This is not
surprising. When asked what to save in a
fire, people routinely list photographs.
Someone rarely suggests that the sixty inch
television should be torn off the wall and
rescued. The photographs might be blurry
or badly cropped with missing heads, but
they serve as a catalyst for memories of
events, people, and emotions.

But, then, why would one care to save the
photographs from previous generations?
There was no personal interaction with
your great-great-grandfather, no associated
memories, or emotions. The images
represent an idealized version of our story
and our origins. Life on a farm in Virginia
in the nineteenth century was probably not
wildly luxurious. I look at a photo of my
great-great-grandfather and imagine a

rural life with fresh vegetables, healthy
living, and people reading by the firelight at
night. [204] This is entirely fabricated. I
invented the narrative from the books I
read, films I saw, and stories passed down.
Nostalgia, here, serves a purpose. It is
reassuring that our life is not dull drudgery,
going from day to day with the same events.
It tells us that life is part of an extended
narrative with adventures, love, anger,
meaning, and ultimately hope that we will
also be remembered.

The photograph itself, as an artifact and
historical record, is contradictory. First, we
assign emotional value to a printed photo.
Regardless of the owner, few people enjoy
burning photographs (except at the end of a
relationship to serve as a way to delete the
past). Like a book, even if it belongs to
someone else, there is emotional weight and
ownership attached to the photograph itself
as profoundly personal and valuable.

Black-and-white photography or film
reframes history and memory. [205] While
high-resolution color images may engage
the viewer more deeply, soft or grainy
black-and-white photographs allow for the
manufacturing of a personal narrative.

204

205

FEATURES · SERIES

03.08.94
TUESDAY
7:00 PM
CENTRAL LIBRARY
FREE

G
C
S

GUEST CURATED SERIES

filmforum

SCRATCHING THE BELLY OF THE BEAST
CUTTING EDGE MEDIA IN LOS ANGELES 1922–94

206

207

REPRIEVE AT KAUTON's Painted especially for Harolds Club, Reno by Charles Wysocki

208

STAGECOACH RACE TO CARSON CITY Painted especially for Harolds Club, Reno by Nick Galloway

206
Portfolio of Paintings, Nevada, The First Hundred Years book
Harolds Club
1964

207
Reprieve at Ragtown lithograph
Charles Wysocki
1964

208
Stagecoach Race to Carson City lithograph
Nick Galloway
1964

209
The Adventures of Huckleberry Finn book cover
Jessica Hische
2011

209

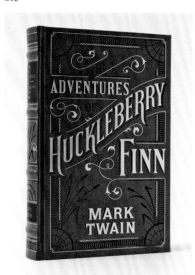

As a tool to engage nostalgia, the photograph (a physical artifact, not a digital screen-based image) is especially potent. It is a record of another time and place filtered through the point of view of the photographer. Without being consciously cognizant, the viewer determines who the photographer might be and where he or she is standing in relation to the subject. This forces the viewer to imagine him or herself in the scene. That connection creates an emotional response that signals feelings such as loss, sadness, pleasure, anger, frustration, or confusion.

Tapping into this healthy and positive emotion is an enormous benefit in marketing and advertising. As such, designers incorporate cues that convey nostalgia. Here, design connects to the idea of the past, not reality. The illustrator Paul Detlefsen began his career painting backdrops in Hollywood. He transferred the skill of creating fictitious narrative scenes to a career in calendars and lithographs. [203] A range of manufacturers applied his work to jigsaw puzzles, cards, prints for the home, and other items. These were enormously successful throughout the 1950s and 1960s to an audience who had endured the uncertainties of the Great Depression and World War II. Now faced with the Cold War, the rise of suburbanization and isolation, changing family systems, rigid social rules, and globalization, they longed for the security of an earlier time.

Images of an unspoiled pre-urban America gave the viewer a sense of security and hope, with longing for simpler times. They are oversaturated pristine landscapes missing telephone poles or crowds. Many include a boy with a straw hat and his dog, referencing Mark Twain's *The Adventures of Tom Sawyer* or *The Adventures of Huckleberry Finn.* [209]

A promotional item for the centennial of the statehood of Nevada, presents an idealized image of the American West in the nineteenth century. [206–8] Here, stagecoach races are exciting, but not life-threatening. Saloon girls are loud, but no doubt quite proper when pressed for other services. And silver miners work hard together in the mines to strike it rich. This is not the reality seen on television programs such as *Deadwood* or *Westworld*.

210
Vuiton Cabinet
d'Écriture typeface
collection
Jean Francois Porchez
2009

211
Cinzano Bitter poster
Nicolas Diulgheroff
1928

212
L'Arte del Gelato
packaging
Louise Fili
2009

213
Penguin Books
Great Ideas,
Volume 1 book covers
**Jim Stoddart,
Phil Baines,
Catherine Dixon,
Alistair Hall, and
David Pearson**
2013

There is no senseless murder, horse manure in the streets, or women forced into prostitution and abuse. The scale of the lithographs is essential. They are typically small and personal, no larger than twelve inches wide. These are not grand landscapes with heroic vistas. The size engages the viewer personally and individually.

A designer must work with the viewer's knowledge and associations without taking a hard turn past nostalgia into sentimentality, which is overemotional, lacking any reality, and hackneyed. The best examples preserve the connection to truth and historical knowledge. Jean Francois Porchez's typeface collection Vuitton Cabinet d'Écriture for the French luxury brand Louis Vuitton Malletier is equally flawless. At first glance, the collection appears to be a set of Vuitton typefaces from the early twentieth century. They feel exotic and elegant, and recall grand travels on the Nile or the Orient Express. However, Porchez designed the collection in the early twenty-first century exclusively for Vuitton bespoke stationery and personalized writing materials. {210}

Regardless of the typographic knowledge of the viewer, Vuitton Cabinet d'Écriture reminds the viewer of a different time. We recognize the cues: a formal condensed script, letterforms based on 1920s signs in Paris with elements such as a lower center bar of the *E*, and the extended sans serif. This is not because one is an expert on the typography of 1920s France, but because one has had exposure to these graphic elements in films, photographs, and stories. Porchez avoids an overly sentimental aesthetic with highly refined forms, exceptional quality, and expertise on typographic history.

In the 1980s, Louise Fili stepped away from the cold and impersonal approach of Swiss International Style modernism. She initiated a new postmodern approach to typography that celebrated a warmer and more decorative past. As an author of countless books, Fili introduced the design industry to the elegance and timelessness of typography previously dismissed as out of style. Italian design of the 1920s {211} inspired the solution for L'Arte del Gelato, a Sicilian gelato shop in New York. {212}

Without an understanding of Italian, any viewer immediately recognizes the product type. The script letterforms, coral and peach color palette, and delicate forms encourage the customer to imagine great gelato shops in Sicily in the 1930s. The approach encourages the viewer to refer back to a time before mass production of food, when handmade ingredients and quality mattered. And to imagine a *passeggiata* by Marina di Riposto with pistachio gelato.

David Pearson's superb cover designs for *Penguin Books Great Ideas* series embody artistic fidelity. The covers are not glaringly themed. The typographic choices, classic typefaces such as Caslon, Bembo, Bodoni, and Baskerville, relate to the book's content and the era of the first printing. Pearson's philosophy reveals itself with the solution, "Many prophesied the death of the printed word, but we see it as an opportunity to luxuriate in the craft and tactility of the physical book and the printed page." {213}

KitchenAid recognized the consumer's demand for a return to healthier cooking and introduced a line of mixers with a nostalgic aesthetic. The pastel colors suggest baking and cooking in the 1950s,

210

ER
HANDMADE PENS
Les fabricants de bons produits
Calligraphy is the most fundamental element of art
Paper & Ink
Paul Colin
Your Charming Love Letter
MODERNE
Cabinet d'Écriture
Stylos à encre
PLACE SAINT-GERMAIN DES PRÈS
SUR-MESURE

211

212

213

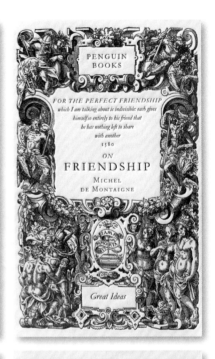

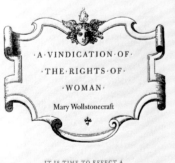

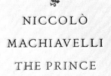

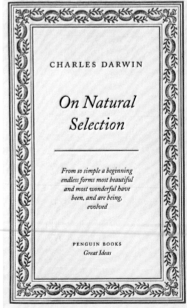

Virginia Woolf
A Room of One's Own

A woman must have money and a room of
her own if she is to write

Penguin Books · Great Ideas

MARCUS AU
RELIUS·MED
ITATIONS·A
LITTLE FLES
H, A LITTLE
BREATH, AN
D A REASON
TO RULE AL
L—THAT IS M
YSELF·PENG
UIN BOOKS
GREAT IDEAS

Let the ruling
classes tremble at
a Communistic
revolution.
The proletarians
have nothing to
lose but their
chains.
They have a world
to win.
Working men of all
countries, Unite!
The Communist
Manifesto
Karl Marx &
Friedrich Engels

Penguin Books Great Ideas

ST AUGUSTINE
CONFESSIONS
OF A SINNER
AS A YOUTH
I HAD PRAYED TO YOU
FOR CHASTITY AND SAID, GIVE ME
CHASTITY
CONTINENCE
BUT
NOT
YET

PENGUIN BOOKS · GREAT IDEAS

SIGMUND FREUD

CIVILIZATION AND

ITS DISCONTENTS

PENGUIN BOOKS
GREAT IDEAS

Civilization overcomes the dangerous aggressivity of
the individual, by weakening him, disarming him and
setting up an internal authority to watch over him, like
a garrison in a conquered town

FRIEDRICH
NIET3SCHE
WHY I AM
SO WISE

I know my fate. One day there
will be associated with my
name the recollection of
something frightful   of a crisis
like no other before on earth, of
the profoundest collision of conscience.

Penguin Books   Great Ideas

214

215

and like the L'Arte del Gelato packaging, a time without processed food, multiple chemicals, and mass-produced ingredients. Whether we had the kinds of mother or grandmother who baked cookies, cultural references tell us that a mother using this appliance in 1955 probably made cracker-jack cookies or meatloaf. The pastel colors inspire the consumer to use it and replicate a wholesome and healthy experience for his or her family. {214}

Winter Milk is committed to fresh and natural lactose products: ice cream, milkshakes, and frappés. Anagrama's design solution references Mom and Pop ice cream shops in the 1960s rather than adopting a corporate big chain approach.

The crisp orange and white palette, vintage shapes, and plain-spoken typography suggest a place to find handmade food. {215, 216} The restraint here is the key to the design's success. Like Porchez's Vuitton Cabinet d'Écriture type collection, Anagrama worked with minimal elements without running over the line to cartoonish and "funny retro."

Nostalgia makes us comfortable. There is no "shock of the new." We recognize something in the solution, even if we do not have an exact reference. The design is welcoming and suggests reassurance. When I launched the online publication, *Burning Settlers Cabin,* I designed an identity and visual system. Shortly after I tired of the identity and developed a different logo. I began to question the standard belief of one logo for a brand. Why not one hundred?

The logos proliferated to become an extensive library of versions. While all are original, there is a common theme of nostalgia. The logos reference extinct attractions at Disneyland and Walt Disney World, films of the 1960s and 1970s, European signs, and Victorian publications. The marks appear friendly, familiar, and unthreatening. By reassuring the reader that the content of the site is positive and approachable, I could address a range of subjects, some not polite. {217, 218}

Malibu Shirts produces vintage-replica and original designs. Their retail environments showcase one of the most comprehensive collections of historic surfing memorabilia in the world. The objective is to preserve

216

214
Artisan® Series 5
Quart Tilt-Head Stand
Mixer
KitchenAid
2017

215, 216
Winter Milk branding
Anagrama
2017

218

217

219

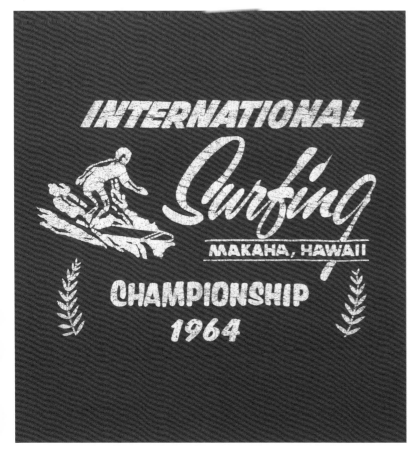

217, 218
Burning Settlers Cabin
branding
Sean Adams
2008–19

219
Malibu Shirts
Makaha 64
**Jeff Jensen and
Denny Moore**
2018

and promote Polynesian artifacts and surf culture. Researchers searched for one-of-a-kind trophies, photos, surfboards, film footage, magazines, and vintage clothing for design concepts. By reproducing graphics with surf pedigree, the brand not only educates the consumer but puts surfing history into his or her hands. As with other successful solutions utilizing nostalgia, Malibu Shirts succeeds with respect for the audience's intelligence and commitment to the history of the subject.{219}

Places connect to a narrative and time. Ask someone about specific cities, and he or she will imagine a story and time: romance in Paris at the turn of the twentieth century (the belle epoque), Berlin in the 1920s, as

decadent and dangerous, or New York and its speakeasy parties in the 1930s. California occupies a place in the public's mind built on myth and storytelling. Ask a person in Shanghai, Melbourne, Moscow, or London to describe California, and he or she will talk about palm trees, endless sunshine, surfing, movie stars, and swimming pools. Yes, these things are in California, but the nostalgia omits the reality of daily life and the complexities of millions of other stories.

Designers work with iconography based on nostalgia. All forms of design need to communicate an idea quickly, and the fastest route is recognizable icons. Whether

the viewer has visited a place or not isn't relevant. What we see on television and film, or read in books and magazines provide symbols and metaphor as a language. {220–225} For example, a visitors' map to California looks like California. The image of the coast and the Pacific Ocean is apparent, but the dominant element is the typography to convey the message. The 1970s "groovy" letterforms might live on a van, and are repeated to evoke a sunset. A painting by Alfred Bierstadt from 1866 portrays Yosemite Valley as heaven. Even the backdrop of the fictional Hollywood apartment of *I Love Lucy* shows the Hollywood sign in the distance, reinforcing the nostalgia of a place and time that never existed in reality.

220
Merced River,
Yosemite Valley
Alfred Bierstadt
1866

221
Jack in the Box
restaurant sign
photographer
John Margolies
1977

222
Puzzle Sputnik
Chandelier
Jonathan Adler
2018

223
UCLA Summer
Sessions poster
Sean Adams
1998

224
Faithfully reproduced
Hollywood living-
room set from
television program
I Love Lucy
Carol M. Highsmith
2018

225
California
visitor's map
unknown
2015

220

221

224

222

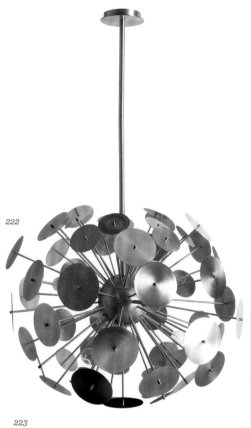

223

UCLA Summer Sessions 1998
www.summer.ucla.edu

225

OFFICIAL CALIFORNIA VISITOR MAP

Chapter 11: Anger

Anger, or hate? Hate is directed to an individual or group. You "hate" someone or a group of others who you believe is "bad." This is someone you believe has done or may do bad things to you or your community. Anger is what you feel about a specific action or set of actions: "I'm angry that you ate the last of the ice cream." Both emotions served a purpose functionally. Anger informed individuals how to behave and what a community deemed appropriate. Hate, while unpleasant, gave us a reason to avoid someone negative for the community. Anger is what you feel to punish or a banish an individual harming the whole. One can be angry at a spouse, parent, child, or friend and still love them. If you hate someone, you're probably angry too.

226

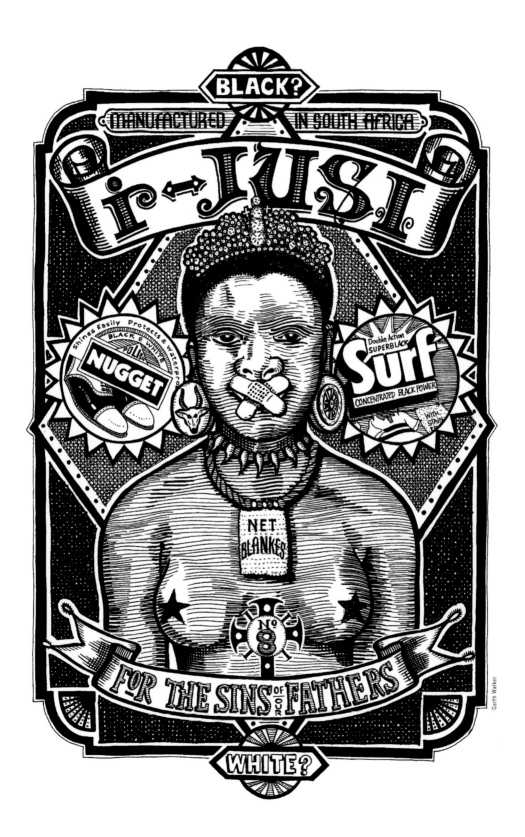

Garth Walker

226
Black and White:
i-jusi magazine
Garth Walker
1999

227
Security camera
footage from Hibernia
Bank robbery and
Patty Hearst: Tania
broadside
possibly Symbionese
Liberation Army
1974

227

When a person feels anger, brain activity focuses attention. This provides the ability to focus on an issue until its resolution. If a person is anxious, he or she will also focus more deeply. Anger is often at the root of anxiety. One is anxious about the test and probably resentful that it is required. I am anxious that my stomach is upset, and angry at the restaurant *and* cook. Anger, as an emotion, is effective as a mnemonic tool. Events tied to strong emotions are imprinted more indelibly as memories.

There is an old saying in advertising, "When you teach a donkey a trick, step one is to hit it across the forehead with a two-by-four board to get its attention. Do the same with an audience." Anger is that two-by-four board. If a design can provoke anger, it has the audience's attention. The viewer is now prepared to hear a command, take action, or find information.

For an issue of *i-jusi*, focused on South Africa's racial issues, Garth Walker designed a cover with the force of that two-by-four. The high contrast and visceral image represents silencing, consumerism, forgiveness, and guilt. {226} Walker does not gently tip-toe around the issue, but faces it directly. The image's power derives from its

form and the natural response to imagine oneself as the subject — censored, stripped naked, enslaved, and presented as a commercial product.

In February 1974, a leftist urban guerilla group, self-named the Symbionese Liberation Army, kidnapped nineteen-year-old Patricia (Patty) Hearst. The group locked Hearst, grand-daughter of billionaire William Randolph Hearst, in a closet and brainwashed her for over two months. In April, Hearst issued a statement, "I have been given the choice of being released in a safe area or join the forces of the Symbionese Liberation Army and fighting for my freedom and the freedom of all oppressed people. I have chosen to stay and fight. I have been given the name Tania after a comrade who fought alongside Che [Guevara] in Bolivia for the people of Bolivia." Two weeks later, she and the Symbionese Liberation Army robbed a branch of Hibernia Bank in San Francisco.

Supporters of the criminal behavior and counterculture protesters used the poster of "Tania" holding a semiautomatic rifle in front of a logo of the SLA. as an icon for revolution. {227} The poster was a reminder

229

228

230

228
Free Angela Davis
Now! poster
**New York Committee
to Free Angela Davis**
1971

229
Kent State: Avenge
poster
unknown
1970

230
Wanted, The Student
as a Potential Assassin
student-published flyer
unknown
c. 1968

231
Broadside for
the Capture of
John Wilkes Booth,
John Surratt, and
David Herold
unknown
1865

231

of Patty Hearst's conversion from a comfortable upper-class student to a radical criminal for the revolutionary cause. The subtext is that if she can change sides and take action, so can you. This is a moral story to anyone following the same twisted sentiment including the martyrdom of the group's leaders. It energizes that audience to action with anger against the "establishment." Like the Walker illustration for *i-jusi*, the aesthetic is raw. Here, the poster is also spontaneous with low production quality; this is a revolution, no time for good printing. The blunt imagery and typography in all capital letters, tells us that "Tania, the revolutionary" is fighting for the "people".

In 1970, during a Vietnam War protest, National Guard soldiers fired into a group of unarmed students, killing four and wounding nine others. John Filo, a Kent State photojournalism student, photographed Mary Ann Vecchio kneeling over the body of Jeffrey Miller. The hand-scrawled command "Avenge" weaponizes the photograph. {229} Another poster, of political activist Angela Davis also commands the viewer to take action. {228} Like the Tania poster, the gritty, intense,

and passionate language on these posters distinctly transmit this information: the event that occurred is inexcusable, the only emotion to feel is rage and anger, the action must occur immediately, there is no time to refine anything, there is no money behind this issue that can produce change, it is the responsibility of the masses, and you, to act.

A flyer depicting an image of President Lyndon B. Johnson showing a scar presents a visual language of psychedelia and handmade antiestablishment graphics. The content describes a student's experience with the United States Secret Service after writing, "Johnson's war in Vietnam makes America puke." Agents told the student he was being investigated because the statement was interpreted as a threat to assassinate President Johnson: "If enough people puked on the President, it would kill him."

Anger here is interpreted through the lens of a generational divide. To a person under thirty in 1968, the handwritten headline, low-quality images and production, and centered typography signaled a rejection of corporate and International Swiss graphics. This was not Madison Avenue Helvetica selling Pontiacs. {230}

232

232
La lutte continue
poster
Atelier Populaire
1968

233
La chienlit c'est lui!
flyer
unknown
1968

234
Provoke & Beyond:
Hong Kong
International Photo
Festival poster
Wang Zhi-Hong
2018

233

This language of anger and protest, raw images, blunt typography, and inexpensive materials or printing traces back to "wanted" broadsides from the nineteenth century. Printers created the broadsides with wood type and one-color printing. Wood type is lighter than metal type forms, enabling larger scale letters. But, as wood objects, they lack refinement and detail. The printer did not make aesthetic design choices; the form is the result of resources. With only a certain number of letters, a printer chose the typeface for size and quantity of letters. If one only had two *E* letters, he or she chose another typeface for the words, "The Murderer." Crude typography and printing is apparent on a poster for the capture of John Wilkes Booth and others conspirators for the assassination of President Abraham Lincoln. The raw vernacular suggests immediacy, action, and anger. {231}

Two posters speak to the striking workers and students during the May 1968 uprising in France. They display the same crude vernacular as the Kent State poster, but make statements rather than an explicit command. "La lutte continue" (The struggle continues) encourages the protesters to remain enraged and fight. The

raised fist has been a symbol of resistance since the beginning of the twentieth century. By the 1960s, the Black Panther Sisters (women's liberation) and other groups adopted it. Here, it is attached to a factory, representing the workers. {232}

A second poster from May, 1968 uses a representation of General Charles de Gaulle and phrase "La chienlit c'est lui!" During the protests, de Gaulle angrily used the term as a pun, "La réforme oui, la chie-en-lit non." This translates as, "Reform, yes—shit in bed, no." The student protesters co-opted the statement and reframed it as, "The shit in bed, it is him!" The play on words and cartoonish symbol of de Gaulle served to minimize de Gaulle's power and image, reminding the viewer that he is part of the "other," the enemy. {233}

While these examples focus on political activism and revolution, anger is also a potent tool creatively. The 2018 Hong Kong International Photo Festival featured the exhibition *Provoke & Beyond*. *Provoke* magazine, founded in 1968, subverted traditional aesthetics of photography with "grainy, blurry, out of focus" images. The mainstream, shocked and angered by the disruption of "correct" standards, villain-

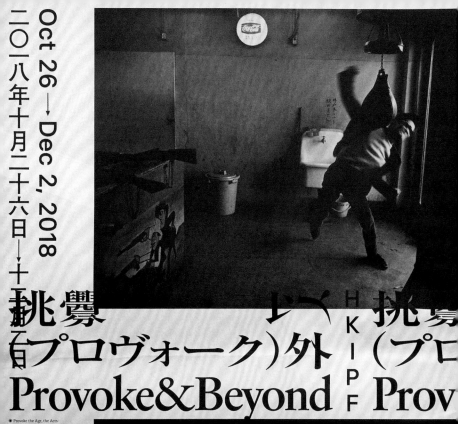

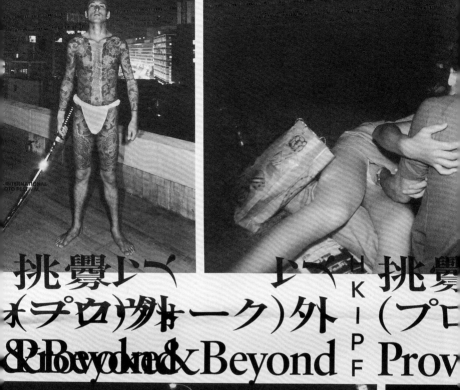

挑釁いく
（プロヴォ）ー外
&Beyond Beyond K I P F Prov

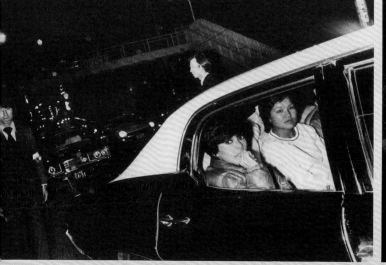

235

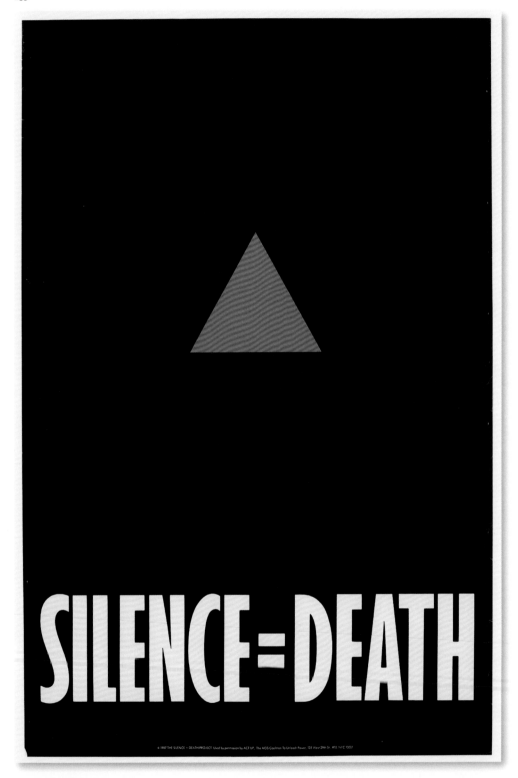

236

235
Silence=Death poster
Avram Finkelstein
1986

236
Read My Lips flyers
Gran Fury
1988

ized and persecuted the four founders of the magazine. It ceased production after three issues. The magazine's message, however, influenced Japanese photographers for the next 50 years. {234}

The designer Wang Zhi-Hong refused to censor or sanitize any of the magazine's intense photographs and minimize their impact. The images are unsettling and, at the same time, aesthetically beautiful. The result for the viewer is a set of contradictory emotions from anger to fascination and finally, revulsion.

The AIDS crisis in the 1980s affected men and women globally. Governments did little, preferring to ignore the pandemic as it afflicted populations of LGBT and people of color. Peaceful resistance proved to be useless here. ACT UP (AIDS Coalition to Unleash Power) demanded action, medical research, treatment, and legislation to address the disease. In 1986, Avram Finkelstein created the Silence=Death logo to combat institutional silence of HIV/AIDS. The poster appropriated a pink triangle, used in concentration camps by Nazis to identify homosexuals.

Finkelstein turned the triangle upside down, reclaiming the icon and conveying the anger and fight necessary to combat the issue. {235}

Gran Fury, the creative group that designed many of the additional graphics, incorporated modern branding and mass marketing strategy to spread the message. Like the May 1968 French uprising graphics, the remarkable success of the Gran Fury work lies in its lack of overt commands. The use of statements, "Read My Lips," taken from a speech by President George H. W. Bush, forced the viewer to consider the issue and, therefore, become engaged. {236}

The idea of "the other" is at the core of ACT UP's call for a voice and action. In this instance, the other is a group outside mainstream society not adhering to the social contract of marriage, family, and reproduction. As social animals, people construct tribal communities. Anyone or any group that threatens the community is, in fact, a threat to the object of love. The threat is often represented by the existence of others: immigrants, homosexuals,

criminals, different races, and those with opposing political or religious views. Anger and hate develop once the threat is identified.

Expanded economic models from the industrial revolution, spurred by scientific discovery, led to the nineteenth-century impulse to categorize and measure everything. Measuring the human body is not a new idea; ancient Greeks associated ideal proportions with divine harmony. But in the nineteenth century, criminology turned to human metrics and pseudo-science. If one could determine a common shape and size of a criminal's nose, forehead, mouth, and head, perhaps these could point to an evolutionary identification. Individuals who shared physical features with criminals were thought to be inherently bad and not to be trusted or allowed to participate in the mainstream society in any capacity.

With the introduction of photography, nineteenth-century police departments collected vast and disorganized "rogues' galleries" with portraits of criminals. It was near-impossible for a police officer to locate an individual image among the thousands of mug shots.

237
Notation of Scars,
Schematic Drawings
Alphonse Bertillon
1893

238
Fiche anthrpométrique
data sheet
Alphonse Bertillon
1893

239
*Tableau synoptic des
traits physionomiques:
pour servir a l'étude du
"portrait parlé"* poster
Alphonse Bertillon
1909

238

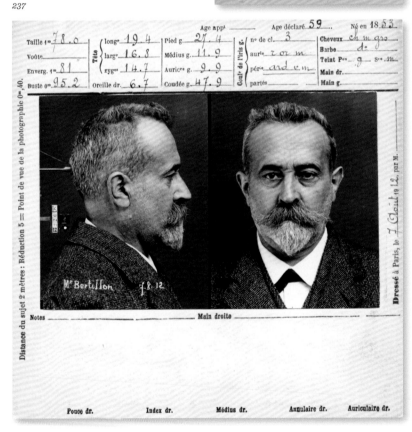

237

A police clerk in Paris, Alphonse Bertillon, developed a system of classification based on human metrics. While he wasn't interested in identification of a possible criminal based on facial features, Bertillon did see a more practical use of the measuring process. He devised a photographic system of portrait *parlé* (the spoken portrait) that detailed measurements of the face and body. {237} The photographs and metrics divided the male criminal's face into unique units of information. {238, 239} From these, Bertillon devised a system to better identify repeat criminals. His system, known as Bertillonage, introduced practices to the criminal justice system, that are still utilized today.

If the goal is to create an environment of enmity on a nationwide scale, the designer must portray the enemy as beyond redemption, entirely alien to our values, and inhuman. During World War II, both the Allied and Axis powers represented the enemy as subhuman. It is more difficult to be angry and hate another human being if we identify with him or her in any way. But, a stereotype caricature is easy to hate and can serve as the subject of our anger with another group.

239

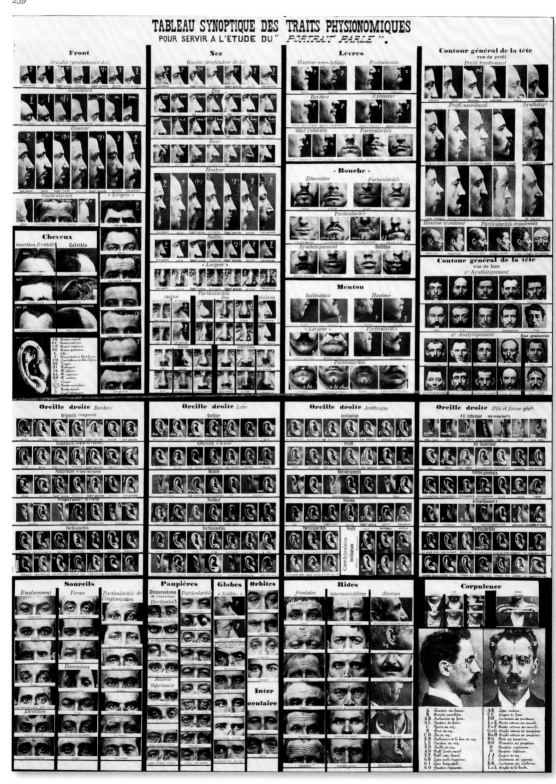

TABLEAU SYNOPTIQUE DES TRAITS PHYSIONOMIQUES
POUR SERVIR A L'ETUDE DU "PORTRAIT PARLE".

240
A nova ordem—do eixo
(A new world order—
the Axis) poster
**Edward McKnight
Kauffer**
c. 1943

241
Soldiers Without Guns
poster
Adolph Treidler
1944

240

The enemy might be shown with animal-like characteristics, typically engaged in reprehensible action harming women or innocent children.

A grotesque poster representing the Axis powers, *"A nova ordem—do eixo"* "A new world order—the Axis," preys on the idea that the enemy is a hideous and inhuman creature with malicious intent. {240} It is far easier to kill another if he or she is not another human being sharing the common goals of all people: to be happy and safe. Conversely, heroic images of actual men and women might be used to represent members of our own community. {241, 242} Rather than represented as cartoon characters, these figures might be realistic, although idealized, images of people in our culture. During World War II, designers applied clear and bold typography, strong patriotic colors, and images of people serving the greater good. These, combined with the heroic stature of the individuals, conveyed the sense of community and reassured us that the intended audience was, indeed, morally correct and backed by God while the enemy was evil.

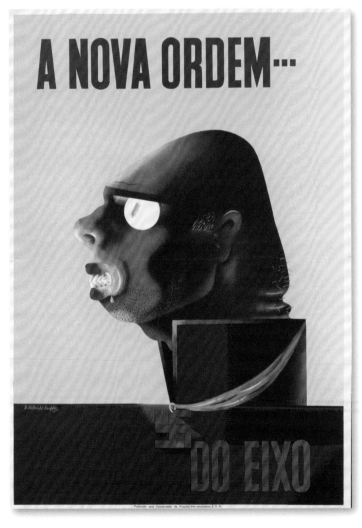

241

242

242
Everything for the
Front. Everything
for Victory poster
El Lissitzky
1942

243
Pvt. Joe Louis poster
**U.S. Government
Printing Office**
1942

244
United We Win poster
**Photograph by
Alexander Liberman**
1943

245
Together poster
William Little
1943

243

244

245

Chapter 12: Pleasure

The same areas of the brain that mediate which foods are desirable and who is attractive as a mate respond to aesthetically pleasing art and design. In the presence of beauty, we feel pleasurable emotions such as wonder, joy, and transcendence. Pleasure allows us to step away from reality. When we are absorbed in a pleasant experience such as an engaging book, movie, or piece of music, or a wonderful meal, we lose a sense of time and place. Consider the power of design here; a positive response to an object is neurologically similar to the fulfillment of basic human survival impulses such as hunger and sex.

246

246
Arizona Inner Space
textile environment
Barbara Shawcroft
1971

247
Private Chapel
Ensemble of Scenes
stained glass in
Ebreichsdorf, Austria
unknown
c. 1390

248
The Harrowing of Hell
detail from stained
glass window

As a primal and powerful force, pleasure is regulated. As human beings, we spend enormous resources and time seeking the sensation of pleasure in many forms. To affirm or deny pleasure is a forceful management tool for any political, religious, or social organization. [247, 248] If one group or government can control this primary human motivation, it can control most behaviors. While each society defines which types of enjoyment are acceptable and which are unacceptable, there are commonalities in how all social groups regulate pleasure. According to neurologist David Linden these include:

» Pleasure must be sought in moderation,
» Pleasure must be earned,
» Pleasure must be achieved only through natural and wholesome means,
» Pleasure is fleeting,
» Denying pleasure will yield spiritual growth.

In his book *Designing Pleasurable Products* Patrick Jordan identifies four types of pleasure. Physio-pleasure is associated with the physical body and our senses:

touch, taste, smell, and sexual and sensual pleasures such as the "new car" smell, or a wonderfully soft duvet cover. Socio-pleasure is the happiness we feel from interaction with others. Will people approve of my bumper sticker? Will my family appreciate the drinks from the espresso machine? Psycho-pleasure sounds like a disturbing film (or a good one) depending on one's taste), but this is our cognitive and emotional response, the pleasure gained from the accomplishment of a task: I can understand the Ikea instructions to build the Billy bookcase. And finally, ideo-pleasure connects to our values and aspirations, such as purchasing the first edition of a rare book or hanging a poster that confirms our beliefs and values.

Pleasure is also profoundly subjective. Some people enjoy being bound while others find it intolerable. But, positive physical sensations tend to have broad appeal. Barbara Shawcroft's environmental experience *Arizona Inner Space* conceived the structure to be a continually growing and changing organic shape. As time passed, she planned to add similar forms reached through textile tunnels. The soft

and natural colors evoke the southwest. Light filters into the inside, creating a womb-like contemplative space. The structure is inviting, gentle, and warm, inviting the viewer to enter, relax, rest, and feel pleasure [246].

If I were to install the *Shrine Doors with Indra, Divine Regent of the East* at my house, I would expect my guests to appreciate my taste and, considering their pricelessness, my remarkable wealth. This is an example of socio-pleasure. [249] One feels a sense of pride and confidence from the positive opinion of others. This is a complicated response that integrates the desire for group acceptance, the reinforcement of one's aesthetic judgment, and the ability to obtain financial resources. The doors, made with repoussé silver sheets over intricately hand-carved wood not only tell the story of Indra, but exist for the social recognition of the owner.

Regardless of their intelligence, and no matter what they claim, people prefer ideas and problems that are easy to consider and solve. If a designer creates an impenetrable solution clear only to him or herself, few

247

248

249

249
Shrine Doors with
Indra, Divine Regent
of the East
India, Gujarat
1850–1900

250
Futuro Typojanchi
2015 installation
**Lizá Ramalho and
Artur Rebelo at R2**
2015

251
Futuro Typojanchi
2015 poster
**Lizá Ramalho and
Artur Rebelo at R2**
2015

250

251

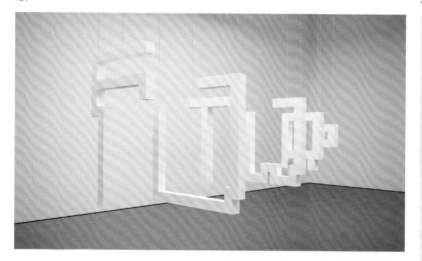

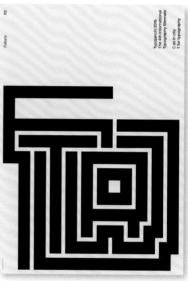

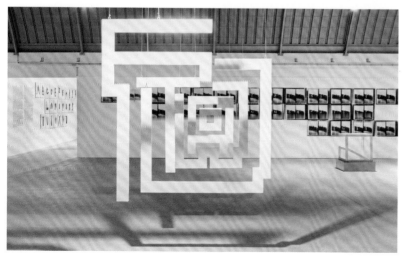

252

252
9 West 57th Street
address sign
**Ivan Chermayeff at
Chermayeff &
Geismar**
1974

people will engage. Those that do will leave
frustrated. But one will feel enormous
pleasure if a complex idea is conveyed in an
approachable way. The Porto design firm
R2 designed a typographic installation that
creates a question and allows the viewer to
solve it. The installation and posters for
Typojanchi 2015, the 4th International
Typography Biennale in Seoul, draw
parallels between architecture, context,
and typography. {250, 251} The viewer has a
sense of accomplishment, with just the
right amount of effort.

This is true also when a viewer follows a
simple idea presented in an unexpected
way. The sign for the Solow Building at 9
West 57th Street in New York represents a
simple idea presented with an unconven-
tional approach. {252} We expect to see the
building number on the building. It might
be in a style and typeface we appreciate or
don't. Chermayeff & Geismar turned the
street address here into a distinctive
two-ton red sculpture. The red color and
thick letterform appear warm and friendly.
Long before the rise of selfies, tourists
routinely photographed each other before
the large numeral, feeling delighted when
they recognized it was a street number.

253
Tupperware Party
industrial film
Tupperware
Corporation
c. 1961

254
Tupperware
Servalier Bowl
Tupperware
Corporation
1984

255
What I Hate poster
Sean Adams
2014

253

 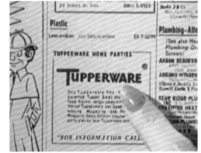

254

Tupperware is an extraordinary example of pleasure driving success. Earl Tupper, a chemist at DuPont, worked with leftover polyethylene to create a reusable and waterproof container for food. It even created a pleasant "burp" when sealed. He launched Tupperware in 1946, and it sat on store shelves, unsold. Brownie Wise saw the potential for Tupperware. Wise recognized the postwar shift of social structures as families moved to the suburbs. Previously living close to neighbors and family in urban apartments, housewives found themselves isolated with no connections. In 1951, Wise initiated the Tupperware party as the only outlet to purchase the product.

The parties provided access for suburban women to meet neighbors. Peddling Tupperware to their neighbors, women could earn money for more independence without leaving the domestic sphere. {253} Tupperware's functional design evolved to include fashionable colors that looked good in the refrigerator, keeping a kitchen neat and well organized. {254} Tupperware introduced a range of products to address suburban entertaining: the Party Bowl, the Pie Taker for transporting desserts, and the Dip 'n Serve Serving Tray.

255

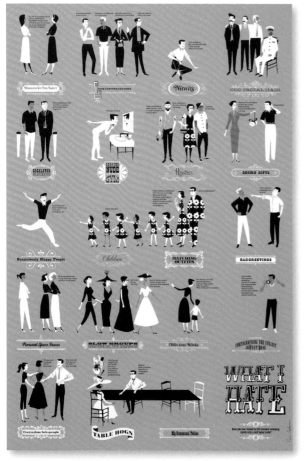

Have you ever wanted to kill someone annoying slowly with a dull butter knife?

"DESIGN" GIFTS

Hipsters

Overzealous Salespeople

256
The Miller House
**Eero Saarinen and
Alexander Girard**
1953
Photograph:
Carol Highsmith (opposite)
Balthazar Korab (below)

256

Sharing our beliefs and finding others that agree with them provides pleasure. It reinforces our self-identity as being part of a community and confirming that we were, indeed, correct all along. In 2014, the Wolfsonian Museum in Miami exhibited a group of posters regarding complaints. The relatability of the many issues strengthened the visitor's belief that others agreed with his or her ideas. I designed a poster with a light and pleasant tone that, at first glance, appeared fun and innocent. The pink background, illustrations, and multiple decorative typefaces hid the negativity. Titled *What I Hate* the individual complaints included issues such as matching outfits on yelling children, people blocking the path at the top of an escalator, groups of people walking four abreast along a sidewalk, and other social problems. {255}

In 1953, Eero Saarinen designed the Miller House and Garden in Columbus, Indiana, for the American philanthropist J. Irwin Miller and his wife, Xenia. The Millers requested a house to entertain large groups and heads of state. The result was a 6,800 square foot modernist residence. Alexander Girard's interiors for the house effortlessly combined modernism, comfort, rigor, and a multitude of patterns and textures. One of the great designers of the twentieth century, Girard refused to follow the strict and cold guidelines of hard-line modernism. He introduced color, unexpected proportions, and the human touch with folk art. The pleasure of seeing and holding an object made by hand can't be overstated. The Miller House's conversation pit served as the warm heart of the house. Guests descended into an intimate space filled with a remarkable amount of pillows.

Girard also designed a fifty-foot storage wall of bookcases, cabinets, alcoves, and empty spaces for Miller's collection of objects. At the time of its design, following Mies van der Rohe's principals of "less is more," folk art and assorted objects would have been considered an excessive and irrelevant decoration. Girard embraced the fine line between "more is more," and excess. In the Miller House, however, the richness of the materials and objects provided physical pleasure, social pleasure, and the joy of aesthetic beauty. {256}

And then there is the type of pleasure that drops below refinement and civilized behavior. In the *King James Bible*,

When Moses was grown, he refused to be called the son of the Pharaoh's daughter, choosing rather suffer affliction with the people of God than to enjoy the passing pleasures of sin.

There is a long history of pleasure as sin: if one is to reach the divine, one must suffer without expectation of reward. Americans are a product of split personality driven by the clash of two groups.

In 1607, three ships, *Susan Constant*, *Discovery*, and *Godspeed* arrived in Virginia. The English built a fort and founded Jamestown. A large part of the crew and subsequent settlers were English nobility and gentry, typically second or third sons who would not inherit a property in England due to laws of primogeniture. These people came to Jamestown to find their fortune and enjoy life.

In 1620 the *Mayflower* arrived at Plymouth, Massachusetts. These settlers came to America to avoid religious persecution as Puritans. They founded a colony based on piety and ethical Christian values practiced by the entire community. Four hundred

257
Booze book
**John Astrop and
Eric Hill**
1967

257

years later, these two strains coexist in the national character. Pleasure is good and not sinful, or pleasure is sin, and suffering brings one closer to God. The result is a guilty conscience. To work around that, advertising has promoted hard work and reward. For example, the McDonalds slogan, "You deserve a break today," tells the hardworking parent that it is acceptable to take the family to McDonald's rather than cook dinner. The message brilliantly merges the two national characters: you work hard, so now you can enjoy yourself.

Drinking, sex, and other pleasurable activities deemed illicit require a light touch (no pun intended) in design. Too heavy-handed, and the message can read as disturbing and off-color. The *Booze* book is an example of both a time when excessive drinking was acceptable, and judgment-free and there was a light approach to pleasure. {257} The book of cocktail recipes includes a variety of comical illustrations by John Astrop and Eric Hill. Quirky headline typography signals levity in the book. Granted, there are stereotypes such as the Irish bartender and flower children hippies, but the overall effect presents alcohol not as a damnable vice leading to hellfire, but as added spice for a party.

Design that appeals to our physical senses is powerful and calls on our primal sensual pleasures. Alternatively, asking the viewer to feel pleasure intellectually is more challenging. Designing for a series of architecture lectures must attract the viewer and promise a reward of knowledge. The acquisition of information is important, but provides less primal satisfaction and pleasure than finding and owning an object one covets. Kobi Franco's poster for a series of architecture lectures at Azrieli School of Architecture in Tel Aviv, promises vital information. The design promises an intellectually robust experience, but Franco's poster also assures the audience that these lectures are dynamic, multi-faceted, and exciting. Working with the illusion of three-dimensional space, architectural images and elements, and energetic color, Franco created a clear organization of information. The shapes also reinforce the content: architecture and the exchange of ideas. {258}

When we discover something beneficial, we feel pleasure. On the African savannah, the community praised the individual who found the sweetest fruit or a new tool. Contradictorily, shopping should be a stressful process. We are parting with

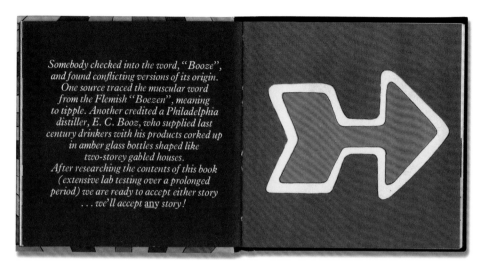

*Somebody checked into the word, "Booze", and found conflicting versions of its origin. One source traced the muscular word from the Flemish "Boezen", meaning to tipple. Another credited a Philadelphia distiller, E. C. Booz, who supplied last century drinkers with his products corked up in amber glass bottles shaped like two-storey gabled houses.
After researching the contents of this book (extensive lab testing over a prolonged period) we are ready to accept either story . . . we'll accept <u>any</u> story!*

Design & Illustration by John Astrop & Eric Hill

IRISH COFFEE

2 jiggers strong, hot COFFEE
1 jigger IRISH WHISKEY
½ jigger COINTREAU
(use brandy instead of cointreau for a less sweet drink)
WHIPPED CREAM

Mix coffee with warmed whiskey and cointreau in Irish coffee glass. Top with whipped cream.

COLD IRISH COFFEE

2 jiggers strong, iced COFFEE
1 jigger IRISH WHISKEY
½ jigger COINTREAU
1 small scoop VANILLA ICE CREAM

*Mix ingredients in blender until smooth.
Serve in chilled Irish coffee glass.*

52

258

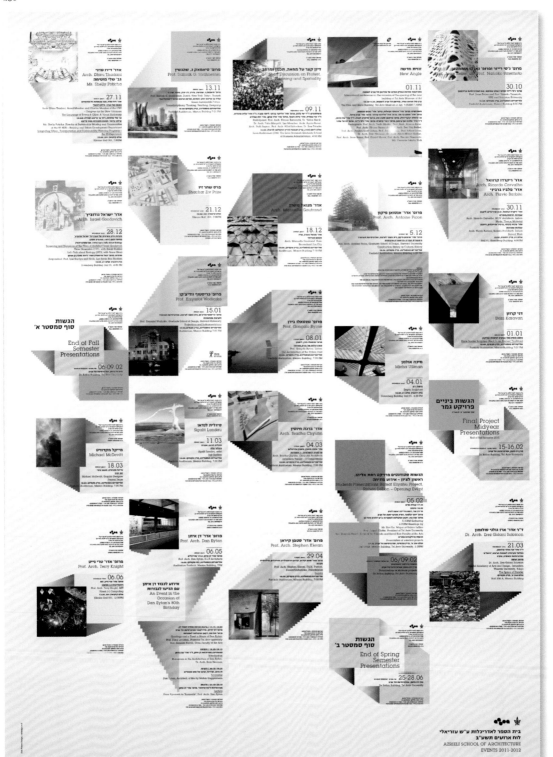

258
Azieli School of
Architecture Events
poster
Kobi Franco
2011

resources in exchange for an item that may or may not meet expectations. But, neurologically, shopping engages our brain in the same region as sex or appetite that produces the feeling of pleasure. We are managing two contradictory sensations. While considering the product, one part of the brain engages expecting the joy of ownership. When contemplating the cost, another section is at work evaluating loss of funds. The expectation of the product providing pleasure mediates with the rational side evaluating cost. When a subject decided to not purchase an item, researchers saw increased activity in the section of the brain that deals with feelings of loss.

A retail experience is more successful if the design raises the positive aspects of shopping: the anticipation of the search, discovery, examination of the product, and pleasure of purchasing it. Simultaneously, a successful retail environment minimizes the negative associations: fighting to acquire a product, confusing navigation, and parting with resources. Anagrama's design for Novelty Apparel in Monterrey,

Mexico maximizes pleasure in shopping. Novelty curates clothing and accessories from international brands. The curated experience amplifies the reward of discovery and minimizes the fear of a "wrong" choice.

Anagrama's forms and colors create a proprietary identity for the brand. The soft pink color reduces stress and serves as a neutral, but friendly, background for the products. [259] Minimal display of the items creates a gallery-like atmosphere reinforcing the curatorial approach. Here, the customer does not need to fight with others over a pile of sale sweaters, or dig through racks of clothes to find a shirt. The tone is inviting and pleasant with no sense of rush or pressure. Not only do these aspects create a favorable shopping experience, they reinforce the sense of belonging to the community who shares the same aesthetic.

Collective enjoyable experiences provide an opportunity to exceed society's regulation of pleasure. In daily life, we moderate our expressions of joy. When a positive event happens, few people jump up and down as if on a television game show. But this

excessive behavior is allowed at a music festival, party, or other group event involving alcohol or drugs. Group hedonism, a term coined by sociologists Gary Alan Fine and Ugo Corte, creates a strong sense of communal identification. When separate from daily life physically, the group bonds with the shared experience of pleasure. This encourages positive relations, collaboration and cooperation, and moderates interpersonal conflict. [254]

As an example, Burning Man is a cultural festival in the middle of Nevada. Over seventy thousand people gather to build a temporary city. The community explores artistic expression through art, architecture, design, music, theater, and dance. The event culminates in the burning of a large wooden effigy of a man. [261] The meaning of this action and the enormous temporary effigy is never explicitly made clear. Each visitor to Burning Man may determine the nature of symbolism or metaphor (if he or she is still conscious).

259

260

259
Novelty Apparel,
Monterrey branding
and retail design
Anagrama
2013

260
Biombo con desposorio
indígena y palo volador
(Folding Screen with
Indian Wedding and
Flying Pole)
unknown
c. 1690

261
Burning Man Festival
Bureau of Land
Management
2012

261

Chapter 13: Honesty

In 1902, Mark Twain wrote in his notebook, "Honesty: the best of all the lost arts." Almost 120 years later, we continue to lament the loss of truth in our society, even though we can now access whatever information we require within seconds. News is transmitted twenty-four hours a day globally. At the end of the twentieth century, futurists promised a revolution of democracy. Populations would access truth through the free internet. All governments would lose their stranglehold on their version of the truth once everyone could obtain accurate information. Of course, that didn't happen. Information splintered as it proliferated. Each person is now confronted with information that reinforces his or her existing beliefs. Facts are irrelevant or filtered to suit an agenda that assures us that we are correct in our assumptions.

262

263

262
Advertisement for
Mamiya/Sekor
cameras
Louis Danziger
1968

263, 264
Salk Institute for
Biological Studies
Louis Kahn
1965

264

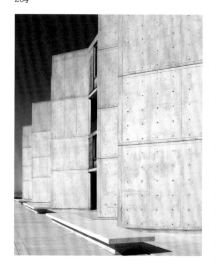

Consumers are aware that he or she is targeted with strategy, research, and psychology to compell them to purchase items. The viewer might have believed a television advertisement in 1960 that promised extra-soft hands with the right brand of dishwashing soap, but few people today would race to the store trusting the message. The noted expert on trust issues D. Harrison McKnight describes dispositional trust as a propensity or tendency to believe in the positive attributes of others in general. To trust that the dishwashing soap will soften one's hands, one needs to think that the manufacturer is honest and fair.

Unfortunately, most people today believe that manufacturers are only manipulating the consumer for fiduciary gain. Honesty is at the core of trust. To trust a design, product, or communication, one expects technical competence; the designer or manufacturer should clearly have expertise and knowledge. We must believe that the solution offered by the product reinforces the natural and social moral order. And we hope for the financial exchange to meet our exigencies.

I stated in a lecture recently, "Change starts with true honesty." When we set aside our pride, preconceptions, and personal narrative, we can judge who we are with honesty. It is vulnerable, to be honest. By exposing the truth, we open ourselves to criticism or, worse, self-judgment. Think of this in the context of design. When the designer strips away any decoration, disguise, or veneer, and exposes the reality, he or she relinquishes control, trusting the viewer to recognize and believe the message. {262} This, however, is precisely what is required for the viewer to engage with a design in a meaningful way.

The ideas of modernism from the Bauhaus spread globally by the 1930s. One of the tenets, truth in materials, reflects the rejection of deception. A metal table looks metal; it is not painted to appear as wood. In design, this is expressed literally, in Louis Kahn's architecture for the Salk Institute for Biological Studies in La Jolla, California. Kahn designed the campus buildings with concrete, lead, steel, and glass, with an open plaza of travertine marble. {263, 264} The raw, unpainted concrete and teak wood is exposed. A line of water runs down the center of the square, seemingly ending in the Pacific Ocean. The result echoes the

265

266

267

268

265
Dress ensemble
unknown
c. 1870

266
Seed stand
unknown
1800–25

267
Shaker rocking
chair
unknown
1820–50

268
Shaker sampler
Mariah Boil
1844

269
*Southern California
Institute of Architec-
ture: Building in
Los Angeles* guidebook
Sean Adams
1995

269

cliffs and coasts of California. As a research institute, the design communicates the beauty of the site, and demonstrates a lack of pretension, and refusal to hide anything.

150 years before the Bauhaus, James and Jane Wardley and Mother Ann Lee founded the United Society of Believers in Christ's Second Appearing, commonly referred to as the Shakers. The Shakers' beliefs, including the goal of perfection in labor, is explicit in Mother Ann Lee's statement, "Put your hands to work, and your heart to God." Making something well was an act of prayer for the Shakers. Furniture, build-ings, textiles, and housewares followed the principles of simplicity, utility, and honesty, while excess decoration represented corruption and vanity. {265–268} Built-in cabinets and simple boxes created places for storage, "A place for everything, and everything in its place." The Shakers' minimal and authentic aesthetic and philosophy influenced architects and designers interested in American pragma-tism, and it merged with Bauhaus modernism in the 1930s and 1940s.

In the mid-1990s, graphic design embraced a "more is more" attitude. Many designers enjoyed layering images on images, overlapping degenerated typography, and applying a multitude of printing effects. In the hands of the originators of the ap-proach, much of the work was stunning. But the majority, designed by imitators, simply communicated chaos and excess. In 1994, the author and architect Aaron Betsky asked me to create a guide to alumni architecture for SCI-Arc, the Southern California Institute of Architecture. {269}

Rather than opting for excess, I looked back to the Shakers, avoiding visual clutter to design a publication stripped of all unnec-essary elements. I wanted to convey the simple truth of the content, the remarkable architectural work. Philosophically, I rejected the chaotic work of the time as elitist if only twelve people with advanced degrees could understand the message. Straightforward and clear typography, two colors with no additional effects, and exposed staples spoke to the viewer with nothing hidden: honestly.

270
Barro de Cobre
packaging
Savvy
2009

271
The Form of Form
graphic system for an
exhibition at the
Lisbon Architecture
Triennale
**Lizá Ramalho and
Artur Rebelo at R2**
2016

270

271

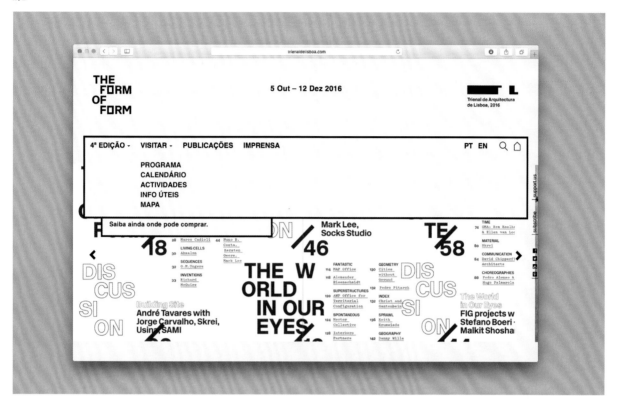

The Mexico City agency Savvy developed a similar approach to the graphic language for Barro de Cobre mezcal packaging. The raw and bare typography, black on white, and straightforward bottle shape read as pure with no requirement for anything to elevate the brand. Here, there is no demand to deceive or entice the viewer. The designers present the product and facts with confidence. Savvy also incorporated the duality behind Barro de Cobre's processes by overlapping different textures and finishes. White glossy paper representing the technical aspect of the product sits on top of a warmer uncoated paper with embossing, serving the handmade. Savvy traced a digital typeface by hand to create the brand's logo,

capturing the slight imperfections that come from doing things by hand, once again communicating the opposing and complementary forces of this mezcal. {270}

The graphic identity for *The Form of Form* at the Lisbon Architecture Triennale {271} follows a logic similar to the brutalist architecture of the Salk Institute. Information is presented with no decoration and a severe black and white palette. Here, the message is about clear and practical information, not enticing photographs that will lure visitors to the exhibition. While this seems antithetical to attracting an audience, R2's solution presumes that the intended audience is sophisticated enough to engage with the content alone. The viewer is not interested in being beguiled into attending the exhibition.

The non-design approach, with broken words and a mix of digital and industrial typefaces, appears to be generated automatically. Uncomfortable negative spaces and a rigid grid structure add to the perception that the structure here on the website is determined not by human design, but as a result of the coding.

The exclusion of human interference to resolve the typographic issues reinforces the veracity of the information. A machine will not lie or exaggerate. It can only present raw data. The viewer is presumed to have an intelligent lack of gullibility. The design is successful because it presents information without any deception.

272
Origen México
book cover
Blok
2016

273
Origen México
book interior

272

Blok's work for *Origen México* similarly steps away from overt design contrivances. *Origen México* is an encyclopedic collection of cultural reference points from Mexico. {272, 273} The content includes information on a range of subjects from the black clay pottery of Oaxaca to filmmaker Alfonso Cuarón. Blok's direct design creates an unbiased representation of the text and imagery. The images are presented candidly. Text pairs with the photographs without interrupting or competing. The result is a matter-of-fact tone that is frank and blunt. The paper exposes Blok's ineffable skill with materiality. Thin sheets allow the viewer to see the content from one side of a page to the back with show-through. This links the entries conceptually to communicate the interconnected nature of Mexican culture.

The idea of honesty in design is controversial. Can design ever be genuinely truthful with no subjective bias? Some designers adhere to the philosophy that a solution should be dependent entirely on the problem presented. The designer is not relevant except to solve the problem for the client with no "personal style." Other designers integrate a personal approach.

273

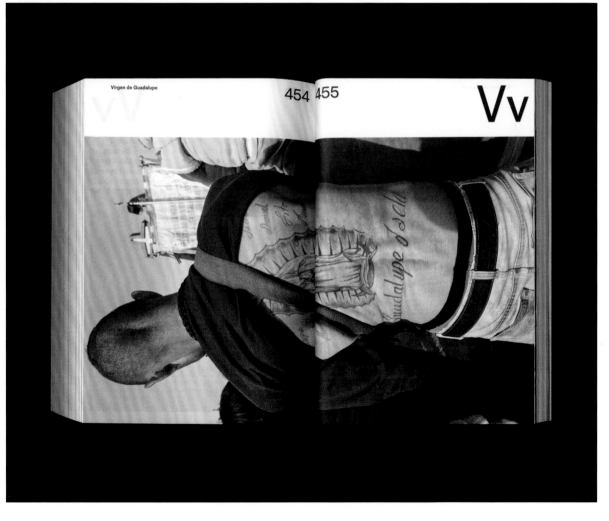

274
Lunar Surface
Photographed by
Surveyor V
**National Aeronautics
and Space Adminis-
tration (NASA)**
1967

275
Bell Centennial
typeface
Matthew Carter
1978

276
The Angry Black South
paperback book cover
Roy Kuhlman
1965

274

275

ABCDEFGHIJKLMNOPQRSTUVWXYZ
abcdefghijklmnopqrstuvwxyz
1234567890

All human beings are influenced by experiences, beliefs, and concepts. It is impossible to create without these aspects shaping the work. To suggest that one can remove any subjective decision making is not credible.

However, we expect certain things to be entirely objective. A map, bus schedule, or telephone book is only about information. One doesn't expect a designer to put his or her "spin" on the content. We hope a syringe or life jacket will do their job with no design ploys that might interfere with the pure function. We trust that scientific, medical, and technical content and products are honest. A photographic print from NASA, a grainy black-and-white image with a small white band of information, communicates the veracity of the picture by its lack of visual sophistication [274]

As seen with both the Wang Zhi-Hong and Blok books, a designer can create a solution with the appearance of objectivity and no individual style. But that is an aesthetic and conceptual choice relying on the skill of these designers. It is not easy to create solutions that are simple and honest. One has no elaborate material, form, or technique to distract the viewer from the

design. Each element must be considered. Anything that does not contribute to the communication is extracted.

Roy Kuhlman's cover for a paperback, *The Angry Black South*, appears effortless and not designed. [276] But the straightforward typography and one-color printing communicates the message with no histrionics or sensationalist imagery. It would be a disservice to the subject, the African-American experience before the Civil Rights Act, to trivialize it with design orchestrations. Maintaining the minimal creates authenticity and confidence that the content is unimpeachable.

Typefaces vary from illegible and elaborate to utilitarian and understandable. Matthew Carter designed Bell Centennial, commissioned on AT&T's anniversary, to solve technological and physical issues. Bell Centennial is the result of function driving all design choices, aspiring to legibility and precise information delivery, without sacrificing beauty. Carter compensated for the thin ink and inexpensive newsprint used for telephone books by incorporating "ink traps." The strokes of the letters come together and fill in with ink, creating a well-formed (not over-inked) message. [275]

276

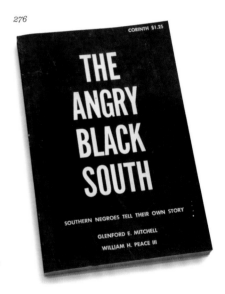

277
Barcelona Chair
**Ludwig Mies van
der Rohe**
1929

278
Barcelona Pavilion
**Ludwig Mies van
der Rohe**
Photographer:
Cemal Emden
1929

277

Mies van der Rohe designed the Barcelona chair for the Barcelona Pavilion in 1929. {278} He saw the pavilion as a way to symbolize the progressive and energetic spirit of the Weimar Republic. The chair adopts classical forms that can be traced to ancient Greece. Mies van der Rohe stripped all extraneous elements from the chair, exposing its construction. The philosophy of an honest chair with a transparent structure for the masses was short-lived. The complicated structure proved challenging to mass-produce. Like most of Mies van der Rohe's architecture, the elegant forms address the requirements of straightforward and minimal design while appearing light and transparent. {278}

Finally, designing less to mean more is the goal of truth in design. For the design of the Sundance Channel, the network's content—independent film—demanded a design that showed respect for artistic integrity. Part of the Sundance brand's mission is to present creative endeavors as they are intended to be seen. There is no censorship or reinterpretation of a filmmaker's work. To add layers of graphic design to the content would change the goal. A convoluted, graphic-heavy solution with flying shapes and typography would suggest a network channel about graphics and flying shapes, rather than independent films. {279}

The solution presents the content with minimal graphic interference. It uses only one typeface, Bob, named after the brand's founder, Robert Redford. It is typeset in all capital letters in one-size-fits-all communications. On-screen, the typography is religiously placed in the center to appear on any form of content: film, photography, and literature. The outcome was an honest and respectful graphic visual system that presented information without impeding the filmmaker's message.

278

279

279
Sundance Channel
broadcast graphics
**Sean Adams and
Samantha Jan Fleming**
2010

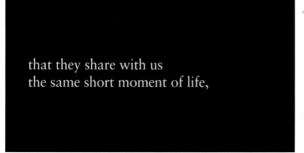

that they share with us
the same short moment of life,

11PM PST/EST   2001: A SPACE ODYSSEY

BATTLESHIP POTEMKIN

SUNDANCE
CHANNEL

NEXT   STRANGER THAN PARADISE

SUNDANCE
CHANNEL

Contributors

Illustration Credits

Every effort has been made to find copyright holders to obtain their permission for the use of copyrighted material. The publisher apologizes for any errors or omissions in the below list and would be grateful if notified of any corrections that should be incorporated in future reprints or editions of this book.

page

6 } collection of the author
9 } San Francisco Museum of Modern Art
10 } The Metropolitan Museum of Art, Gift of Robert Shapazian, 2009
12 } Los Angeles County Museum of Art, Purchased with funds provided by Arthur Hornblow, Jr.
15 } The Metropolitan Museum of Art, Gift of Cythian Hazen Polsky, 1985
17 } courtesy ©Starbucks
18 } The Metropolitan Museum of Art, Edward C. Moore Jr. Gift, 1923
19 } courtesy AIGA
20 } courtesy Herb Lubalin Study Center of Design and Typography
22 } courtesy Paul Prejza
22 } courtesy Paul Prejza
24 } courtesy NASA's Earth Observatory
24 } AdamsMorioka
26 } AdamsMorioka
28 } ©iStock.com/Michael Burrell
28 } ©iStock.com/Adrio
28 } ©iStock.com/Supertramp
28 } ©iStock.com/Spiderstock
28 } ©iStock.com/twilightproductions
29 } images: collection of the author
31 } The Metropolitan Museum of Art, Anne Cox Chambers Gift, 2014
35 } courtesy ©Tecnolumen
38 } Photographs in the Carol M. Highsmith Archive, Library of Congress, Prints and Photographs Division.
39 } courtesy Chermayeff & Geismar
40 } courtesy ©Tecnolumen
40 } Louis Danziger Collection
41 } ©Herman Miller
41 } Louis Danziger Collection
43 } courtesy Stockholm Design Lab
44 } courtesy spillmann echsle architekten
46 } Louis Danziger Collection
47 } The Metropolitan Museum of Art, Gift of Mary and Dan Solomon, 2016
47 } courtesy Richard Danne
48 } Louis Danziger Collection
48 } collection of the author
48 } ©iStock.com/urbanbuzz

49 } courtesy Cooper Hewitt, Smithsonian Design Museum
49 } ©Herman Miller
51 } courtesy ©IBM
53 } ©Vitra
54 } The Metropolitan Museum of Art, Gift of William Church Osborn, 1949
55 } The Metropolitan Museum of Art, Josephine Bay Paul and C. Michael Paul Foundation Inc. Gift, Charles Ulrick and Josephine Bay Foundation Inc. Gift, and Fletcher Fund, 1967
57 } The Metropolitan Museum of Art, Alfred Stieglitz Collection, 1949
59 } Louis Danziger Collection
60 } collection of the author
61 } Library of Congress, Prints and Photographs Division
62 } courtesy the Estate of Elaine Lustig Cohen
65 } collection of the author
66 } courtesy Anagrama
68 } courtesy Marian Bantjes
70, } The Metropolitan Museum of Art, Gift of Mrs. Richard Riddell, 1981
72 } courtesy Neo Neo
76 } courtesy Jeremy Deller and Fraser Muggeridge
76 } courtesy Zipeng Zhu
76 } AdamsMorioka
77 } courtesy Angad Singh
77 } courtesy Neo Neo
77 } courtesy Ian Lynam
78 } collection of the author
80 } courtesy Pentagram
80 } courtesy Anton Tielemans
81 } courtesy Seymour Chwast
82 } courtesy Pràctica
83 } Louis Danziger Collection
83 } collection of the author
84 } courtesy Guan-Hao Pan
86 } courtesy Lavernia Cinefuegas
88 } courtesy Alexander Isley
89 } Louis Danziger Collection
90 } Office: Jason Schulte Design, Jill Robertson, Rob Alexander, Will Ecke, Gaelyn Jenkins, Jeff Bucholtz
92 } AdamsMorioka
95 } Library of Congress, Prints and Photographs Division
97 } Library of Congress, Prints and Photographs Division
99 } Atelier Brückner
100 } courtesy R2
102 } courtesy Stockholm Design Lab
104 } ©IBM
105 } courtesy Marion Dönneweg
106 } courtesy 123RF, James Steidl

106 } James Lemont Fogg Memorial Library, ArtCenter
106 } courtesy Dallas Museum of Art
106 } courtesy Heritage Auctions, HA.com
107 } courtesy Heritage Auctions, HA.com
109 } courtesy Lucille Tenazas
108 } Louis Danziger Collection
110 } courtesy Hampton Duke
111 } courtesy Buro Uebele
111 } courtesy Pentagram
113 } courtesy ©Knoll
112 } courtesy ©Herman Miller
115 } The Metropolitan Museum of Art, Gift of Samuel H. Kress Foundation, 1958
116 } J. Paul Getty Museum
117 } Royal Satfford, exclusively sold at evazeiseloriginals.com, courtesy Eva Zeisel Originals
118 } The Metropolitan Museum of Art, Rogers Fund and The Kevorkian Foundation Gift, 1955
119 } courtesy Artiva Design
120 } Art Institute of Chicago, Gift of Mr. & Mrs. Arthur D. Dubin
121 } The Metropolitan Museum of Art, Robert Lehman Collection, 1975
122 } courtesy ©Herman Miller
122 } courtesy Michael Vanderbyl
125 } courtesy AIGA
129 } courtesy Jennifer Morla
130 } Louis Danziger Collection
132 } Louis Danziger Collection
133 } Library of Congress, Prints and Photographs Division
134 } The Luckman Partnership, Inc., a Salas O'Brien Company
134 } Library of Congress, Prints and Photographs Division
136 } Library of Congress, Prints and Photographs Division
138 } courtesy Angad Singh
140 } courtesy Steff Geissbuhler
141 } courtesy JohnsonBanks
142 } courtesy Pentagram
144 } AdamsMorioka
144 } The Metropolitan Museum of Art, Gift of John Stewart Kennedy, 1897
147 } courtesy Ian Lynam
149 } courtesy Hueso
150 } Office: Jason Schulte Design
154 } courtesy ©Herman Miller
155 } courtesy Angela Baek
156 } courtesy Kobi Franco
157 } courtesy Kizzy Memami

158 } J. Paul Getty Museum
158 } ©Knoll
158 } ©Herman Miller
159 } ©Knoll
159 } ©Herman Miller
159 } courtesy Norm Architects
162 } courtesy El Vivero
165 } Louis Danziger Collection
166 } Library of Congress, Prints and Photographs Division
166 } The Metropolitan Museum of Art, William Cullen Bryant Fellows Gifts, 2008
167 } ©Herman Miller
168 } Chermayeff & Geismar
169 } courtesy UMA
170 } courtesy Ian Lynam
172 } collection of the author
172 } courtesy Marion Dönneweg
172 } 123RF, Julie Deshaies
173 } ©Vitra
174 } collection of the author
177 } courtesy Marieke Voorsluijs, Club Geluk
176 } courtesy Marieke Voorsluijs, Club Geluk
178 } AdamsMorioka
179 } collection of the author
180 } AdamsMorioka
182 } courtesy Marion Dönneweg
183 } Louis Danziger Collection
185 } collection of the author
186 } collection of the author
188 } collection of the author
189 } courtesy Jessica Hische
190 } courtesy David Pearson
192 } courtesy Jean Francois Porchez
193 } courtesy Louise Fili
194 } ©KitchenAid
105 } courtesy Anagrama
197 } courtesy Denny Moore. Malibu Shirts
198 } Library of Congress, Prints and Photographs Division
198 } The Metropolitan Museum of Art, Gift of the sons of William Paton, 1909
198 } Library of Congress, Prints and Photographs Division
199 } courtesy ©Jonathan Adler
199 } AdamsMorioka
201 } courtesy Garth Walker
202 } Lou Danziger Collection
204 } Lou Danziger Collection
204 } collection of the author
205 } The Metropolitan Museum of Art, Gilman Collection, The Horace W. Goldsmith Foundation Gift, through Joyce and Robert Menschel, 2005
206 } Library of Congress, Prints and Photographs Division
207 } Library of Congress, Prints and Photographs Division
208 } courtesy Wang Zhi-Hong
211 } The New York Public Library, Prints and Photographs Division
212 } The Metropolitan Museum of Art, The Horace W. Goldsmith Foundation Fund, through Joyce and Robert Menschel, 2016
213 } Twentieth-Century Photography Fund, 2009
214 } Library of Congress, Prints and Photographs Division
215 } Library of Congress, Prints and Photographs Division
217 } Library of Congress, Prints and Photographs Division
219 } James Lemont Fogg Memorial Library, ArtCenter
220 } The Metropolitan Museum of Art, The Cloisters Collection, 1986
221 } The Metropolitan Museum of Art, The Cloisters Collection, 1986
222 } Los Angeles County Museum of Art, Gift of Julian Sands in honor of his mother, Brenda
223 } courtesy R2
224 } courtesy Chermayeff & Geismar
225 } collection of the author
228 } Library of Congress, Prints and Photographs Division
230 } collection of the author
232 } courtesy Blok Design
233 } courtesy Kobi Franco
234 } Bureau of Land Management Nevada
234 } Los Angeles County Museum of Art, purchased with funds provided by the Bernard and Edith Lewin Collection of Mexican Art Deaccession Fund
237 } courtesy Louis Danziger
240 } The Metropolitan Museum of Art, Friends of the American Wing Fund, 1966 Gift of Mrs. William R. Witherell, 1953 Purchase, Edward J. Scheider Gift, in memory of Kathleen N. Scheider, and David S. and Elizabeth W. Quackenbush Gift, 2008
242 } courtesy Savvy
243 } courtesy R2
244 } courtesy Blok Design
246 } collection of the author
247 } The Metropolitan Museum of Art, The Horace W. Goldsmith Foundation Gift, through Joyce and Robert Menschel, 2001
248 } ©Knoll
250 } AdamsMorioka
251 } AdamsMorioka

Acknowledgments

This book would not have been possible without the contribution of a talented team of collaborators. First, James Evans who brilliantly first suggested the subject. Emily Angus added her expertise with editing and for the highest standards. Isabel Zaragoza was often the first point of contact with contributors and relentless in her task of gathering rights.

Mario Ascencio and Rachel Julius at the ArtCenter Library, once again, stepped in with access to the Library's remarkable physical and digital collections. Jessica Helfand and Paula Scher were a constant source of inspiration and advice. And, finally, thank you to the faculty and students at ArtCenter for giving me the energy and new ways of thinking while writing this book.

Colophon

This book was written and designed by Sean Adams in 2020.
Emily Angus was the editor. Sentinel and Graphik are the primary
typefaces in the book. Jonathan Hoefler and Tobias Frere-Jones
designed Sentinel in 2001. Egyptian or slab serif typefaces such as
Clarendon designed by Robert Besley in 1845 are the precursors to
Sentinel. Christian Schwartz designed Graphik in 2009. Graphik is
a sans-serif inspired by mid-twentieth century Modernist posters.